A YEAR IN THE
COUNTRY

A YEAR IN THE
COUNTRY

EDITORIAL
Editor-in-Chief **Catherine Cassidy**

Vice President, Content Operations **Kerri Balliet**
Creative Director **Howard Greenberg**

Managing Editor/Print & Digital Books **Mark Hagen**
Associate Creative Director **Edwin Robles Jr.**

Editor **Amy Glander**
Associate Editor **Julie Kuczynski**
Art Director **Raeann Thompson**
Graphic Designer **Courtney Lovetere**
Layout Designers **Catherine Fletcher, Nancy Novak**
Contributing Layout Designer **Jennifer Ruetz**
Editorial Services Manager **Dena Ahlers**
Editorial Production Coordinator **Jill Banks**
Copy Chief **Deb Warlaumont Mulvey**
Copy Editors **Dulcie Shoener (Senior), Ronald Kovach, Chris Mclaughlin, Ellie Piper**
Contributing Copy Editor **Michael Juley**

Business Architect, Publishing Technologies **Amanda Harmatys**
Business Analyst, Publishing Technologies **Kate Unger**
Junior Business Analyst, Publishing Technologies **Shannon Stroud**
Editorial Services Administrator **Marie Brannon**

Editorial Business Manager **Kristy Martin**
Rights & Permissions Associate **Samantha Lea Stoeger**
Editorial Business Associate **Andrea Meiers**

Executive Editor,
Birds & Blooms, Country, Country Woman, Farm & Ranch Living and *Reminisce*
Jeanne Ambrose

BUSINESS
Vice President, Publisher **Russell S. Ellis**

TRUSTED MEDIA BRANDS, INC.
President & Chief Executive Officer **Bonnie Kintzer**

Chief Financial Officer **Dean Durbin**
Chief Marketing Officer **C. Alec Casey**
Chief Revenue Officer **Richard Sutton**
Chief Digital Officer **Vince Errico**
Senior Vice President, Global HR & Communications
Phyllis E. Gebhardt SPHR; SHRM-SCP
General Counsel **Mark Sirota**
Vice President, Magazine Marketing **Christopher Gaydos**
Vice President, Product Marketing **Brian Kennedy**
Vice President, Operations **Michael Garzone**
Vice President, Consumer Marketing Planning **Jim Woods**
Vice President, Digital Product & Technology **Nick Contardo**
Vice President, Financial Planning & Analysis **William Houston**

PICTURED ON THE FRONT COVER:
Red barn and the Mission Mountains, Flathead County,
northwestern Montana **Londie Garcia Padelsky**

PICTURED ON BACK COVER:
Yellow warbler **Ted Busby**
Morning rays shining **Aaron Shaver**
Calf with girl **Debbie Bridges**
Winter scene **David Paukert**

© 2017 RDA Enthusiast Brands, LLC.
1610 N. 2nd St., Suite 102, Milwaukee WI 53212-3906

International Standard Book Number: 978-1-61765-673-6
Library of Congress Control Number: 2016961391
Component Number: 116800009H
All Rights Reserved.

Printed in U.S.A.
1 3 5 7 9 10 8 6 4 2

TABLE OF CONTENTS

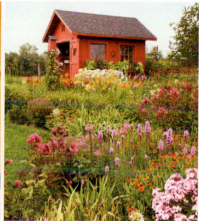

DERRALD FARNSWORTH-LIVINGSTON/WWW.JOURNEYOFLIGHT.COM

Welcome

It's time to take a breath, sit for a moment and lose yourself in the beauty of country life. From fields and farmlands bursting with nature's bounty to prairies and meadows offering a serene escape, America's rural landscape is truly a sight to behold.

In addition to the natural beauty, the values and honest lifestyle of those who live there make these communities all the more special. They are the qualities *A Year in the Country* hopes to share.

This gorgeous keepsake offers a look at the people, places and ideals that strike a chord with all of us. You'll find endearing stories of bustling farms, memories of family pets and animals, recollections of growing up in the heartland and accounts of neighbors who came together to help one another. You'll read about struggles and successes, testaments of faith and fun childhood antics—all shared by those who made the country their home.

Divided by the four seasons, this brand-new book is one you'll cherish all year long. Experience moments of spring awakenings as well as the stillness of warm summer nights. Take a stroll through a brilliant display of autumn photos, and celebrate the winter joys of Christmas in the country.

In addition, you'll find a mouthwatering array of recipes and a sampling of easy crafts at the end of every section. Ideal for bringing the flavors of the season to your table, these farmhouse dishes promise to become favorites in your home, while the simple homespun gift and decoration ideas will certainly nurture your creative side.

Best of all, 304 color photographs offer a visual tour of America's favorite scenery, capturing the heart of this incredible land. Whether you live in or long for the country, this collection is sure to become a treasure you'll savor time and again. We invite you to sit back, relax and enjoy *A Year in the Country.*

Mark Hagen
Managing Editor

Spring

RELISH THE SEASON WHEN NEW LIFE
BLOSSOMS EVERYWHERE YOU LOOK.

DENNIS FRATES

The Good Life

Take a deep breath and smile! This lavender farm is all about helping guests learn, enjoy and relax!

Stop and Smell the Lavender

Simply ask Julie Haushalter how she discovered the lavender business, and she'll say, "I didn't set out to start a lavender business: lavender found me."

In her previous career as a special-needs teacher, school administrator and campus pastor at Eastern Mennonite University, Julie encountered many young people trying to deal with the effects of stress in their lives. So she began researching homeopathic remedies that might manage anxiety.

"Along the way, I discovered lavender," Julie says. "After reviewing the research, I gained a deep respect for the healing properties of lavender."

In 2006 she planted 150 lavender plants on the 25-acre family farm near the town of Weyers Cave in Virginia's Shenandoah Valley. The lavender, a shrub native to rocky mountainsides in the Mediterranean region, thrived, and Julie soon started selling the buds and homemade lavender-based products at a nearby farmers market. Encouraged by the enthusiastic response, she turned White Oak Lavender Farm into a full-time business.

The family now grows more than 9,000 lavender plants in more than 30 varieties that are hand-harvested during the summer months. After harvesting, plants are dried for buds used in teas, baking, sachets and potpourris—and to extract essential oil and floral water, which are used in a variety of bath and body products.

A few years after starting their lavender business, the family expanded it into a thriving agritourism venue when they opened 6 acres of their farm to the public. Their gift shop carries lavender soaps and lotions, handmade sachets, pillows and other gift items; it also sells lavender-infused culinary products like jams and vinaigrettes.

After exploring the farm, visitors can even settle into old-fashioned front-porch rocking chairs to indulge in cups of frosty lavender ice cream.

Out back, the Discovery Area features rabbits, goats, alpacas, miniature horses and other farm animals, as well as a supersized checkerboard, duck pond and therapeutic labyrinth. Guests are welcome to enjoy picnics on the lovely grounds. This is also where they'll find the farm's handsome 1901 barn, drying shed and distillery.

Farm tours and field trips educate about growing, harvesting, drying and distilling lavender. Classes are offered on aromatherapy and making wreaths, halos and wands. Special events include the popular Volunteer Harvest Day, when folks come from miles around to help harvest the lavender.

While Julie is the founder, White Oak Lavender Farm is truly a family affair. Julie's daughter, Rebecca, the head of operations, expanded into wine-making with 1,100 grape vines and a tasting room. Julie's husband, Rick, serves as the farm's financial officer, helps with tours and distilling demonstrations, and keeps the farm looking its best. Julie's parents, Jim and Jessie Walton, helped with harvesting and debudding. And Jessie and Rick's mother, Margaret, sewed the handmade items for the business until they were well into their 90s.

The business also boasts an international component. While on a mission trip in Russia, Julie formed a close relationship with her host family's daughter, Anya Lukyanova, who now helps with the business's international operations. The farm is also working with the Virginia Economic Development Partnership's international trade program.

Julie started her business to help reduce stress, and she says watching people enjoy their experience at the family's farm remains one of her great rewards. "I love to see people arrive, take a deep breath and smile!"

Pat & Chuck Blackley
Staunton, Virginia

Guests love meeting the farm's animals (opposite page, far left), and Julie loves helping them relax (opposite page, center). Volunteer Harvest Day draws lavender lovers from miles around (far right).

Take time to soak in the beauty of spring's miracles, no matter how great or small.

Who Couldn't Use "Cheep" Garden Help?

Last spring, I had a helper that came out of the sky when I began working compost into my small garden. Free labor, if you can believe that.

In the first shovel load, I spotted several small cutworms. These pernicious, pasty beasts were born to devastate gardens. I dispatched the pests and continued digging. But each shovelful exposed more. Soon the capture-and-exterminate routine became tiresome, and a smarter solution came to me. I'd collect them in a container and take care of them all at once, after I finished digging.

I turned to our nearby shed, full of my wife's flowerpots, and returned with a planter the size of a cereal bowl. With each shovelful, I sprinkled cutworms into the planter. Slowly and steadily, I filled the pot.

As I took a rest I noticed a visitor. An inquisitive robin stood on the opposite side of the garden, hopping along the freshly overturned soil. Its eyes focused on me.

When I returned to work, starting down the row from the planter, the robin swiftly moved in. It hopped onto the pot's rim and began dipping its beak inside. Each dip brought forth a wiggling cutworm. Within minutes, the robin had emptied the planter and commenced to stare at me as if asking for more. Thereafter, with each shovelful, I obliged.

We kept at our work until my own stomach signaled for food. I imagined a sandwich waiting patiently on a plate for me inside the house, silently calling for my attention. I returned the shovel to the shed and called it a day, as I had other work waiting that afternoon.

The next morning my feathered friend showed up again, and together we finished the task. It would take months for me to reap any reward for my effort, but the robin seemed quite satisfied with our work.

For weeks afterward, whenever I worked in the garden, the robin would visit. At first, it would hop about in anticipation of another free meal. Then it would become impatient, stomping around like an angry boss who couldn't fathom why the help was so inept. Finally, with no worms forthcoming, it would fly off to a nearby tree, where I imagine it sulked.

But just think how cranky that robin would be if only it knew that for every cutworm I fed it, I hid two earthworms in the soil, saving them from its insatiable appetite and wide-open bill!

William Metcalfe
Arlington, Virginia

Raising Little Squirt

My husband, Shawn, and I enjoy seeing life through the eyes of our five children. It's amazing to watch as they discover their world.

One summer, our oldest daughter, Kaytlin, discovered a baby red squirrel beneath our porch. We watched it from a distance, not wanting to disturb it or scare off its mother. But after a long wait—and looking for traces of a nest or a mother—we realized the tiny squirrel was likely an orphan.

Shaking terribly, he was frail, thin and hungry. We tried to find an expert to help, but we quickly learned there were no wildlife rehabilitators in our county. After some quick research, we concluded that the best way to give the squirrel a fighting chance was to care for him ourselves. We ran to the local Tractor Supply store for puppy formula and other supplies.

More extensive research taught us how much to feed him, how to estimate his age, how and when to wean him, and that we should release him as soon as he could survive on his own.

Our daughters and I shared rotations of feeding "Squirt." Kaytlin took on the most responsibility. She taught him to eat from a syringe, and she woke in the night for his feedings.

To our relief, Squirt soon began to thrive. Within a few weeks he became more alert and active. He would chatter for his next meal, playfully crawl around on the girls and curl up on them for a nap. It wasn't long before he was weaned onto solid food, and we reintroduced him to the wild.

His first few visits to the great outdoors were comical. Just like a child, he would play in the grass some and then run back to Kaytlin for safety. But soon she had him climbing trees and finding nest material.

One day in the trees, he met up with a family of gray squirrels that was none too happy about his visit. They scolded and swatted at him, and he quickly learned some social skills. For several days he played all day in the trees surrounding our house but always came down at bedtime.

And then one night, he didn't. The rain pounded hard, and our girls fretted. But when the sun rose, there was Squirt, begging for a bite to eat. And that remained the pattern for a few weeks.

Squirt became well known in our neighborhood, and visitors knew to be on the lookout for him whenever they stopped by. But mostly he played in the trees, occasionally stopping to swipe snacks from our toddlers, as seen with our son, Chase, in the photo above.

The experience was truly memorable for our children who learned to value and appreciate life.

Rachael Darrah
Dover Foxcroft, Maine

"My daughter, Alexis, is smitten with spring kittens in this photo. Alexis might be only 2 here, but she has a parental look of caring as she cuddles Blacky the kitten at kitty feeding time."
TANYA HANSON
AMERY, WISCONSIN

"The mare's ears perked when she heard the chore time call coming from the barn."
LEONA YODER
SUGARCREEK, OHIO

"Indian paintbrush shows an independent streak in this field of bluebonnets."
MARY LIZ AUSTIN
HAYS COUNTY, TEXAS

"Justine learned about horses the right way, from her cowboy grandpa."
DARANN CURRY
BELGRADE, MONTANA

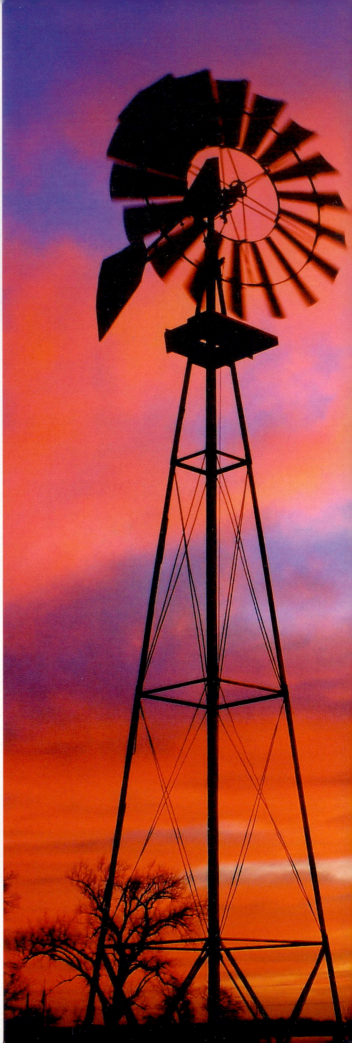

The Song of the Bobwhite

When I was a little girl, I would sit on my pawpaw's old, creaky porch swing with my family, watch the redbirds fly and listen to the bobwhites sing. Some folks know them as quail; country folks know them as bobwhites. I loved to sing the bobwhite song that my grandma Dee had taught me.

"Bobwhite!"

"Peas ripe?"

"No, not quite!"

I wondered why the bobwhite cared about peas, but Grandma said that's what the bird sang, so it must have been so.

As I grew up, I had many other things on my mind, and birds weren't one of them. Many years went by before I finally remembered how much I used to love hearing the bobwhite song. But it was too late. I listened and listened, yet heard nothing. My daddy, one of the smartest men I have ever known, sadly told me that fire ants were disturbing the bobwhites' nests.

Finally, out of the blue one day, my husband, Glen, and I heard a bobwhite! The next time I saw my dad, I told him all about it. The experience brought back so many happy memories.

When Daddy passed away, I took it really hard and asked the Lord for some comfort. Two mornings later, I heard a bobwhite singing. I ran to get Glen, and we went outside and listened together.

A couple of weeks went by. I was still struggling. As I headed out to feed my chickens, that bobwhite was calling his head off again. He sang to me at the chicken pen and continued while I fed and watered. As I was making my way back to the house, I sat down on Glen's trailer and cried.

I stood by the silver maple in the backyard and started whistling the bobwhite song. Sure enough, that bobwhite answered me back! I whistled a few more times, and then I went back into the house, marveling that I had heard a bobwhite call twice in two weeks.

That bobwhite was a perfect gift from the Lord, a comfort to me when I needed a piece of Daddy to hold onto.

Colleen Jackson Goodwin
Livingston, Texas

NORTHERN BOBWHITE: WATERSPIX/SHUTTERSTOCK

The Dreaming Tree

At a passing glance, my favorite old apricot tree might have been dead, except for the riot of pinkish-white flowers sprinkled all over its gnarled limbs. Bits of blue sky showed through the canopy of branches, and a happy bird sang brightly in a neighboring tree. The wind smelled like freshly cut grass mixed with the heady sweetness of the blossoms.

I used to recline in the crook of those tree limbs, my feet tucked in the low fork and my teenage body stretched out along the rough black bark of the sturdy branch that jutted upward at just the right angle.

My brother had a lower branch he'd sprawl on, but I think he was just being gentlemanly by letting me claim that wonderful prime spot.

I'd take my books out there and read for hours, smelling the fragrant promise of apricots and listening to the cows across the pasture. The tree would sing to me, with the leaves and flowers whispering in their own language.

Our apricot trees rarely produced a big crop of fruit. Kansas springs are too unpredictable for constant harvests, but the productivity didn't matter. That special tree was my refuge. I even carved my name into a small branch 20 years ago.

My tree is still standing, although its limbs are darker and much more weather-beaten than when I was a child. It has survived hail, ice storms and winds that seemed strong enough to tear the roof off my house. Yet, every spring it blossoms still.

I'm a grown-up now. I have a job, and I'm mature, responsible, well-respected and busy. There are days when I long for the tranquility of childhood, when I could fling myself into those pink-speckled limbs and forget I was growing up. And though I don't know if I'll ever find the time, I'd love to perch on my branch again, bury my nose into a good book and have the wind gently sing me to sleep once more.

Until then I'll have to hang onto the memory of reclining on that branch under the clear skies, smelling the apricot blossoms and living in every breath.

A.C. Williams
Haven, Kansas

All of God's creatures breathe a sigh of relief upon seeing green pastures and blue skies once again.

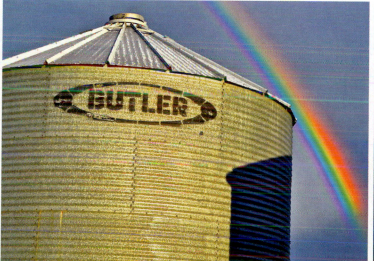

Spring
Scrapbook

SAVOR THE SMILES AND FRESH-AIR MOMENTS OF THE SEASON.

Mountain snowmelt gives
Birch Creek in Idaho a lot
to babble about.
PHOTO BY LELAND HOWARD

Let winter's melting snow reveal a land ready for the return of spring in this delightful photo tour of life in the country.

"Spring is on the way," sings this plump robin spotted in New Jersey.
PHOTO BY STEVE BYLAND/SHUTTERSTOCK

Nothing says winter is over like vibrant Washington tulips and children wading in mud puddles.
PHOTO BY LJ WILSON-KNIGHT/ALAMY STOCK PHOTO

"I caught our son Bridger, watching the horses while we hauled hay."
SUSANNE ROLLER, INDIAN HILLS, COLORADO

"One early spring morning, I noticed this Canada goose with her goslings sleeping comfortably underneath her wing."
JOANNE KILLMER
RINDGE, NEW HAMPSHIRE

"Here's a Hereford cow giving a gentle, encouraging nuzzle to her young calf."
TAMA BAUMGARTEN
BELFIELD, NORTH DAKOTA

Crystal clear Alley Spring
near Eminence, Missouri,
powers a historic mill.
PHOTO BY LAURENCE PARENT

No matter sunrise or sunset, this time of year is a lovely prelude to the glorious summer-kissed days ahead.

"I enjoyed spending a few hours with this ruby-throated hummingbird one afternoon."
JULIA BARTOSH
NOTASULGA, ALABAMA

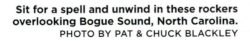
Sit for a spell and unwind in these rockers overlooking Bogue Sound, North Carolina.
PHOTO BY PAT & CHUCK BLACKLEY

This little lady holds a basket for forsythias like a pro in Connecticut.
PHOTO BY TERRY WILD

Cades Cove in Tennessee's
Great Smoky Mountains National
Park is stunning just after dawn.
PHOTO BY PAT & CHUCK BLACKLEY

Daylilies lean toward the sun during a bright day in New York.
PHOTO BY CINDY RUGGIERI

"On a sunny spring day I was cheered by this bright, blooming groundcover."
GERALD YOKELY
TOBACCOVILLE,
NORTH CAROLINA

"Our grandson, Aiden, has a smile that's sweet as a field full of bluebonnets."
JILL DOLLOFF
MIDLAND, TEXAS

It's nearly impossible for any living thing to ignore the beauty that is spring.

"Mom's purrfect peonies attracted the attention of a fine feline."
KAREN DOERSOM
NEWVILLE, PENNSYLVANIA

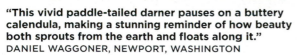

"This vivid paddle-tailed darner pauses on a buttery calendula, making a stunning reminder of how beauty both sprouts from the earth and floats along it."
DANIEL WAGGONER, NEWPORT, WASHINGTON

"While weeding, I saw something scamper under a tomato plant. We have two dogs, so I placed this bundle of cuteness out of harm's way."
BROOK BURLING, WISCONSIN RAPIDS, WISCONSIN

"I was surprised when this Baltimore oriole landed in my crabapple tree instead of at the grape jelly feeder. Who knew I would attract so many colorful birds to our Indiana yard with this lovely tree?"
JOHN ROBERTS
WARSAW, INDIANA

"Each April, I pack a lunch and take my six kids on a tractor ride through the vast tulip fields in Mount Vernon."
DEBORAH CARSON
KENT, WASHINGTON

"This tree-lined lane is pretty nearly all year long."
NANCY PATERLINE
GIBSONIA, PENNSYLVANIA

"I nabbed a shot of these baby calves in Weimar, Texas. They made me rejoice over the beauty and wonder of spring."
DANA SCOTT
PRAIRIEVILLE, LOUISIANA

"This old hay rake looked so pretty in a pasture at the Lupine Festival in Sugar Hill."
MAUREEN GAITES
THORNTON, NEW HAMPSHIRE

"I once captured a moment with a yellow warbler in our backyard during a warm spell."
TED BUSBY
CARLETON PLACE, ONTARIO

"This puppy was our sons' favorite. They played for hours, which even included training him for fieldwork!"
ELLEN GRABER
SHIPSHEWANA, INDIANA

**Spring is blooming at the Wooden Shoe Tulip Farm
in Woodburn, Oregon.**

The end of every spring day signals new beginnings ready to awaken our senses with the rising sun.

Heart & Soul

IT'S A COUNTRY SPIRIT THAT MAKES LIFE WORTH LIVING.

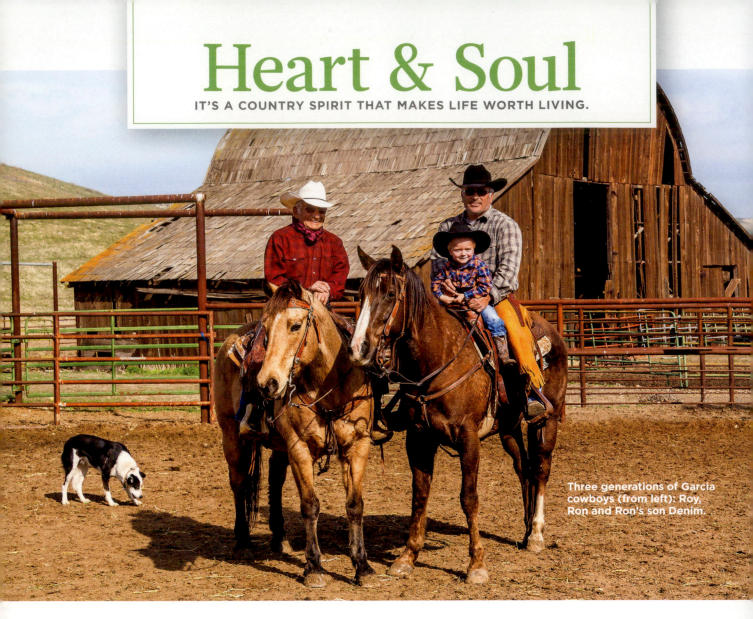

Three generations of Garcia cowboys (from left): Roy, Ron and Ron's son Denim.

A Shetland pony changed their lives in the 1960s and lived in their hearts forever.

Those Bandito Days

He was a Shetland pony, but Bandito wasn't just an ordinary pony. He was a super pony and an honorary member of our family.

Bandito came into our lives when I stopped in Fresno to visit my brother Delmar. He had just returned from the sales yard with a year-old pony. I went into the backyard, and upon seeing this new pony immediately got hold of a long rope, attached it to his halter and started working with him.

I soon learned that he was willing to do everything I asked him to do, so I asked Delmar to sell him to me for my 4-year-old son, Ron. Del agreed at once.

We moved everything to one side of the old Dodge pickup bed to make room for the pony. To my surprise he jumped right up into the bed as if he wanted to go home with us. I tied him in, and we fixed two-by-fours around the side to help him keep his balance.

When we got back to San Luis Obispo, my son Ron hopped on and started riding him. The pony reacted as if he had been ridden all his life.

Ron and his friends had a lot of fun with the shetland. They rode him through the house and up and down the stairs.

The boys loved to run up from behind and spring onto his bare back, the way they did in the old cowboy movies. But the pony always played a trick on them. As soon as the boys jumped up he would duck his head, and the boys would slide down his neck and over his ears to the ground. I think he was having as much fun as they were.

On Halloween Ronnie dressed like Zorro and took his pony trick-or-treating. They rode right up to front doors and knocked. Folks loved it, and Ronnie returned home with saddlebags full of candy and carrots—as well as a name for his pony. That day, the kids called the pony "the bandit," so Ronnie began calling him Bandito.

It wasn't long before Ron was running poles and barrels and doing gymkhana events on Bandito—and winning most of them. He didn't ride like a child; people said he rode like an old man who had been born on a horse.

It was fun to watch Bandito, a 10-hands-high pony, race through the poles. His yellow mane was about 6 inches long, and it always stuck straight up; his tail of the same color stuck straight out, and his big brown eyes were wide open.

One weekend when I was away, Ron asked his mother to take him to a gymkhana. I had taken the trailer with me, so Ron loaded Bandito into the station wagon. He opened up both back doors, took the seat out and led the pony up into the car, closing both doors. Bandito stood sideways, with his head facing out the window on the left side and his tail hanging out the window on the right side.

As Ron excitedly told me later that night, his mom parked right in front of the gates next to the arena in Edna Valley. When Bandito jumped out of the station wagon he made quite the grand entry. He made a pretty grand exit, too. On the way home Ron shared the front seat with his mom and the all-around trophy. Ronnie was so proud of the pony standing quietly in the back of the car.

We had Bandito for 28 years. He was a member of our family and a great partner for Ron, his siblings and their friends. That pony changed our lives. I became the president of the riding and roping club made up of parents and children who had horses to ride. Over the years we organized several trail rides and campouts for children. When I see these people 40 years later, they remember Bandito and the club.

Ron, who was a champion roper and won many events, is raising a pony for his own 3-year-old son, Denim. He hopes this pony, which Denim named Lady Bug, will be another Bandito. But Denim has been riding with his dad all his life and seems to prefer the big horses.

I am 90 years old now and sometimes shed a tear when I think of the Bandito days. We buried him on our ranch up on the hill in the shade of an old eucalyptus tree. Every time I ride by, I think of the super days when we had this super pony with us and he carried Ronnie wherever he went.

Roy Garcia
San Luis Obispo, California

Every day was an adventure for Ron and Bandito (photos lower left, in the 1960s). Ron hopes his buckaroo, Denim, here, finds a friend in his pony, Lady Bug.

The Line Fence

About a month after we moved to our 50-acre farm, I got home from my job as a machinist to find that two of the neighbor's cows and a calf had wandered through the sagging fence along our woodlot.

The neighbor, Lorne Wright, took it all in stride, and he showed up with his border collie, Laddie—to herd them back into his pasture—and with part of a roll of nine-wire fence.

"There's probably enough to reach from the road to the first brace post if you were of a mind to fix this spot," he said. My face lit right up. I wanted to be a good neighbor, but money was tight.

I took some vacation the next week and was well into the miserable job of pulling the old fence out of the tall grass when our mail carrier stopped his car and walked over. Bill Risk was a big, good-natured man who always seemed to have a story to tell. He said, "Fixing fence, are you?

"A long time ago, back when my granddaddy lived hereabouts, two fellows homesteaded next to each other. Back then, you put up fence before you did anything else, so these two men agreed that each would start building fence on opposite ends of their properties and meet in the middle.

"When they finished, one said to the other, 'Well, it looks good. It should last a long time.'

"But the other said, 'My half looks good because I started where I should have, but you started about 2 feet over on my property, and I want it moved now!'

"Well, sir, these two fellows, who could have been good neighbors, started right off with hard feelings. Neither would go to a threshing if the other was there. They even began going to different churches, and the feud went on for years. Finally one man sold his farm, and no sooner had the new owner moved in than his neighbor paid him a visit.

"He said, 'There has always been a problem with our line fence. Your half begins 2 feet over on my property. It should have been moved a long time ago.'

"The new neighbor glanced at the fence, thought for a moment, then said, 'I intend to be here a long time, and I always intend to be a good neighbor. If you think the fence is on your property, you move it to wherever you think it should be, and you'll never hear a complaint from me.'

"They became good friends, went to the same church, threshed together and played cards at each other's homes. And the fence was never moved.

"So keep that fence straight, neighbor," Bill concluded. Then he walked back to his car, leaving me with a smile on my face as I went back to work.

The story had a good moral to it. Whether it was actually true, I never knew. But I did heed the tale. Lorne and I became friends, and stayed friends, for more than 30 years until he passed away.

C.W. Tiffin
Chatham, Ontario

Small Town, Big Miracle

We were city people until about five years ago. At that time, my husband, Jeremy; our 12-year-old son, Holden; and I were all battling cancer. The struggle of illness and raising our four children helped us make the decision to move back to my hometown in rural Nebraska to be near my parents.

Holden did not let brain cancer slow him down. He jumped right in to help his grandpa and learned all he could about running the farm. He even opened his own sweet corn business. I'm proud to say that he won third place in proficiency at the state FFA convention.

When the cancer returned for a third time, the neurosurgeons deemed it inoperable. Research brought us to a doctor at Boston Children's Hospital who said she was confident she could remove the entire tumor. But our insurance would not pay for the operation, and grief and devastation engulfed us.

Word spread, and help arrived quickly. Holden's FFA adviser and our county 4-H leader banded together and decided to hold a fundraiser. They asked us how much money was needed, and I said $39,000 was the cash payment the hospital had agreed upon. It seemed like an impossible number.

The day of the fundraiser was icy and blustery, but people poured into the school, bid on the auction items and ate a warm meal. Volunteers were everywhere, from schoolchildren to retirees. A freewill donation box filled up with checks. It was such an incredible experience.

A couple days later, I got a phone call with news on the fundraiser's success. Our itty-bitty town of only 1,000 people collected over $45,000 in one afternoon.

I am sharing our story because I am humbled and amazed. Our community banded together to make an impossible task possible. Cancer-free two years later, Holden is still working on the farm and helping feed the world, playing football and volunteering with his FFA chapter. He is very proud to be a blood donor and carries his donor card everywhere.

We will never leave our little town or the people who saved our son. And I will always believe in miracles.

Michelle Bruce
Franklin, Nebraska

FENCE: GAIL GRIFFIN; HOLDEN: JULIE SHANNON

Holden's community gave him hope and support when he needed it most.

Food for the Soul

Karl Unnasch says his artistic talent took root under a pool table on the family dairy farm in Pilot Mound, Minnesota. When he was a boy, he crawled under the billiard table one day, looking for a little peace and quiet from his five siblings, and he noticed that the underside was nice, smooth slate.

"I thought, that's just like a chalkboard. So I got a piece of chalk and a wet rag, lay on my back and began drawing," he recalls. "When I finished one drawing, I'd erase it and start another one."

About the same time, Karl began to appreciate relics of bygone days that he found on the farm. "They had history to them," he recalls. "I dreamt about what some rusty part or broken shard was used for, and I imagined all kinds of interesting things I could make out of those pieces."

Everything came together in 2010, and the course was set for something amazing. By then, Karl had become a celebrated sculptor and stained-glass artist. When he was asked to create a piece for the Minnesota Biennial Exhibition, he thought back to all the hours he had spent chisel plowing and disking.

"The cab of the tractor became a place for me to think and process information," he says. "It was a kind of sacred space for a farm kid. You're learning skills that are turning you into an adult, whether you like it or not. You're sloughing off your childhood fantasies and incorporating some adult perspectives, because you're doing an adult job—running a high-powered piece of equipment."

At the same time, Karl says, his head was also filled with movies, TV and comic books. "With these stained-glass windows, I wanted to pay tribute to farm people, ideas and icons, as well as all the fantasy characters that kept me awake while I was driving the tractor back and forth."

Karl borrowed his father's Farmall 966 and created *Near-Mint Condition,* a heroic tribute to country boys. The stained-glass panels on the tractor include Bilbo Baggins, Abe Lincoln, Pa Ingalls, Luke Skywalker, and Clark Kent casually lifting a tractor with one hand—all country boys who livened up his daydreams while he drove up and down the field.

After the success of his tractor-based project, Karl created *Ruminant (The Grand Masticator)* in 2013 to pay tribute to the farmer, food and agriculture. The 6600 John Deere combine and its 34 stained-glass panels explore how food is harvested and processed, and how art is pondered and enjoyed by its viewer.

"We are ruminants of visual language in the same manner as a cow is of its feed or a combine is of its crop," he says.

The set of panels on the corn head showcase a series of traditional rural hand tools from Eric Sloane's book *A Museum of Early American Tools.* Karl plays with the concept of chewing in the cab's stained-glass panels, led by a man chomping into an ear of sweet corn on the front window.

The combine also pays homage to other famous farm-oriented artwork, including panels inspired by one of Thomas Hart Benton's WPA murals; Batman and Robin in a victory garden from a 1943 comic book; and a cartoon version of Grant Wood's *American Gothic.*

Ruminant is now on permanent display at Harvest Park in downtown Reedsburg, Wisconsin.

"Creating these one-of-a-kind pieces of art was like having a serious type of fun," Karl says. "People love to see them, and that just increases my wonderment of seeing them enjoy this work."

Bill Vossler
Rockville, Minnesota

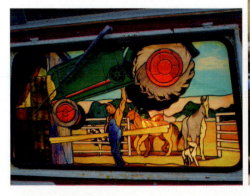

Karl (right) borrowed Dad's 966 to create this tribute to country boys, including Clark Kent (below) and others.

Karl's tractor illuminates more hereos, while his combine (below) celebrates the farmer, food and agriculture in its very own park in downtown Reedsburg, Wisconsin.

Endless hours of daydreaming in a tractor cab now fuel this artist's whimsical storytelling style.

Our Trike-Riding Rooster

A sickly Easter chick found hope and love in our little girl's care.

One Easter, our youngest girl, Jeanne, came home with a baby chick. Her friend Kathy said she could have it, and Jeanne wanted permission to keep it. We lived in the city and had no place to raise a chicken. But a quick assessment of the chick revealed that it was a very sickly little thing, so I agreed, thinking that it likely wouldn't live very long anyway.

I hadn't taken Jeanne's kind-hearted older siblings into account. Before I knew it, they made a home for the chick out of a cardboard box and began nursing it back to health. It thrived in their care, and soon the chick and Jeanne were inseparable. She named it Johnny Rooster after her friend across the street.

It quickly outgrew the box, and we moved it to a cage in the garage at night. But during the day that chick followed Jeanne around like a puppy. It would even ride with her on the handlebars or rear step of her tricycle. They were inseparable.

For some reason, our neighbors never objected to having a chicken wandering around. We lived on a dead-end street without much traffic, but what little there was always yielded to Johnny Rooster. The bird crossed the street at will, and cars always slowed down to let him pass.

Then, one morning about 3:30 a.m., we awoke to an alarming strangling sound. After listening closely, we realized that Johnny Rooster was now indeed a rooster and learning to crow! That presented an entirely new problem. He'd had his annoying moments, such as the time he ate the seeds we had just planted. But that didn't affect the neighbors. Crowing early in the morning would be more than we could expect them to tolerate.

Surprisingly, no one complained. But the problem had to be resolved, and one weekend an opportunity arose. Jeanne came in crying that Johnny Rooster had pecked her. I seized the moment and suggested that perhaps he was ready to live on a farm. She didn't object, so we all piled into the car and drove out to the country before she could change her mind.

We lived north of Milwaukee in Glendale, Wisconsin, with farmsteads all around us. Driving into the first one we came to, we offered Johnny Rooster to the farmer, and he was happy to take him. We said our goodbyes and assured Jeanne that her rooster would be happy there. She had a sad look on her face but seemed content.

Since then, Jeanne has had a long succession of pets and enjoyed a close rapport with all of them. She loved them, and they loved her. But none has been so noteworthy as Johnny Rooster.

Delores Peterson
Spring Hill, Florida

Jeanne and Johnny were an inseparable duo.

A Taste Of Spring

ENJOY THE FRESH FLAVORS THIS SEASON OFFERS.

Traditional Hot Cross Buns

PREP: 25 MIN. + RISING • **BAKE:** 15 MIN. + COOLING • **MAKES:** 2½ DOZEN

INGREDIENTS

- 2 packages (¼ ounce each) active dry yeast
- 2 cups warm whole milk (110° to 115°)
- 2 large eggs
- ⅓ cup butter, softened
- ¼ cup sugar
- 1½ teaspoons salt
- 1 teaspoon ground cinnamon
- ¼ teaspoon ground allspice
- 6 to 7 cups all-purpose flour
- ½ cup dried currants
- ½ cup raisins
- 1 large egg yolk
- 2 tablespoons water

ICING

- 1½ cups confectioners' sugar
- 4 to 6 teaspoons whole milk

DIRECTIONS

1. In a small bowl, dissolve yeast in warm milk. In a large bowl, combine eggs, butter, sugar, salt, spices, yeast mixture and 3 cups flour; beat on medium speed until smooth. Stir in currants, raisins and enough remaining flour to form a soft dough (dough will be sticky).

2. Turn onto a floured surface; knead until the dough is smooth and elastic, for about 6-8 minutes. Place in a greased bowl, turning once to grease the top. Cover with plastic wrap and let dough rise in a warm place until doubled, about 1 hour.

3. Punch down dough. Turn onto a lightly floured surface; divide and shape into 30 balls. Place 2 in. apart on greased baking sheets. Cover with kitchen towels; let rise in a warm place until doubled, 30-45 minutes. Preheat oven to 375°.

4. Using a sharp knife, cut a cross on top of each bun. In a small bowl, whisk egg yolk and water; brush over tops. Bake for 15-20 minutes or until golden brown. Remove from pans to wire racks to cool slightly.

5. For icing, in a small bowl, mix confectioners' sugar and enough milk to reach the desired consistency. Pipe a cross on top of each bun.

Asparagus and Red Pepper Frittata

PREP: 20 MIN. • **COOK:** 25 MIN. • **MAKES:** 6 SERVINGS

INGREDIENTS

- 12 fresh asparagus spears, trimmed
- ½ teaspoon plus 3 tablespoons olive oil, divided
- 10 large eggs
- 3 large egg whites
- ¾ cup whole milk
- ½ cup shredded Parmesan cheese
- ¾ teaspoon salt
- ½ teaspoon pepper
- 1 package (20 ounces) refrigerated shredded hash brown potatoes
- ½ large sweet red pepper, julienned
- 3 fresh basil leaves, thinly sliced
- ½ cup shredded pepper jack cheese

DIRECTIONS

1. Place asparagus on an ungreased baking sheet; drizzle with ½ teaspoon oil. Bake at 400° for 10-12 minutes or until tender, stirring once.

2. In a large bowl, whisk the eggs, egg whites, milk, Parmesan cheese, salt and pepper; set aside.

3. Heat 2 tablespoons oil in a 12-in. ovenproof skillet over medium heat. Add potatoes and press down lightly. Cook, uncovered, for 6-7 minutes or until bottom is golden brown. Drizzle with remaining oil; turn over.

4. Pour egg mixture over potatoes. Cover and cook for 9-11 minutes or until nearly set. Arrange asparagus and red pepper over top. Sprinkle with basil and pepper jack cheese.

5. Broil 3-4 in. from the heat for 2-3 minutes or until eggs are completely set. Let fritatta stand for 5 minutes. Cut into wedges.

Honey Hydrator

START TO FINISH: 5 MIN.
MAKES: 8 SERVINGS (1 CUP EACH)

INGREDIENTS

- ½ cup lukewarm water
- ½ cup honey
- ½ teaspoon salt substitute or ¼ teaspoon salt
- 2 cups cold orange juice
- 5 cups cold water

DIRECTIONS

Place water, honey and salt substitute in a pitcher; stir until blended. Stir in juice and cold water. Refrigerate until serving.

Quiche Pastry Cups

PREP: 30 MIN. • **BAKE:** 15 MIN. • **MAKES:** 1½ DOZEN

INGREDIENTS

- 1 package (17.3 ounces) frozen puff pastry, thawed
- 4 large eggs, divided use
- 1 cup plus 2 tablespoons half-and-half cream, divided
- 1 tablespoon minced fresh thyme
- ½ teaspoon salt
- ½ teaspoon pepper
- ¼ teaspoon ground nutmeg
- 1½ cups shredded Gruyere cheese
- 1½ cups chopped fresh spinach
- 1 medium sweet red pepper, chopped
- 8 bacon strips, cooked and crumbled

DIRECTIONS

1. Preheat oven to 400°. On a lightly floured surface, unfold puff pastry. Roll each sheet into a 12-in. square; cut each into nine squares. Place in ungreased muffin cups, pressing gently onto bottoms and up sides, allowing corners to point up.
2. In a small bowl, whisk 3 eggs, 1 cup cream, thyme and seasonings. In another bowl, combine cheese, spinach, red pepper and bacon; divide among pastry cups. Pour egg mixture over cheese mixture.
3. In a small bowl, whisk the remaining egg with remaining cream; brush over pastry edges. Bake 15-18 minutes or until golden brown. Remove to wire racks. Serve warm.

Mediterranean Shrimp Orzo Salad

START TO FINISH: 30 MIN. • **MAKES:** 8 SERVINGS

INGREDIENTS

- 1 package (16 ounces) orzo pasta
- ¾ pound peeled and deveined cooked shrimp (31-40 per pound), cut into thirds
- 1 can (14 ounces) water-packed quartered artichoke hearts, rinsed and drained
- 1 cup finely chopped green pepper
- 1 cup finely chopped sweet red pepper
- ¾ cup finely chopped red onion
- ½ cup pitted Greek olives
- ½ cup minced fresh parsley
- ⅓ cup chopped fresh dill
- ¾ cup Greek vinaigrette

DIRECTIONS

1. Cook orzo according to package directions. Drain; rinse with cold water and drain well.

2. In a large bowl, combine orzo, shrimp, vegetables, olives and herbs. Add the vinaigrette; toss to coat. Refrigerate, covered, until serving.

Garden Chickpea Salad

START TO FINISH: 25 MIN. • **MAKES:** 2 SERVINGS

INGREDIENTS

- ½ teaspoon cumin seeds
- ¼ cup chopped tomato
- ¼ cup lemon juice
- ¼ cup olive oil
- 1 garlic clove, minced
- ¼ teaspoon salt
- ¼ teaspoon cayenne pepper

SALAD
- ¾ cup canned chickpeas, rinsed and drained
- 1 medium carrot, julienned
- 1 small zucchini, julienned
- 2 green onions, thinly sliced
- ½ cup coarsely chopped fresh parsley
- ¼ cup thinly sliced radishes
- ¼ cup crumbled feta cheese
- 3 tablespoons chopped walnuts
- 3 cups spring mix salad greens

DIRECTIONS

1. For dressing, in a dry small skillet, toast cumin seeds over medium heat until aromatic, stirring frequently. Transfer to a small bowl. Stir in tomato, lemon juice, oil, garlic, salt and cayenne pepper.

2. In a bowl, combine chickpeas, carrot, zucchini, green onions, parsley, radishes, cheese and walnuts. Stir in ⅓ cup dressing.

3. To serve, divide greens between two plates; top with chickpea mixture. Drizzle mixture with the remaining dressing.

Apricot Ginger Mustard–Glazed Ham

PREP: 15 MIN. • **BAKE:** 2 HOURS • **MAKES:** 16 SERVINGS

INGREDIENTS

- 1 fully cooked bone-in ham (7 to 9 pounds)
- ½ cup apricot halves, drained
- ½ cup stone-ground mustard
- ⅛ cup packed brown sugar
- 2 tablespoons grated fresh gingerroot
- 1 tablespoon whole peppercorns
- ½ teaspoon sea salt
- ½ teaspoon coarsely ground pepper

DIRECTIONS

1. Preheat oven to 325°. Place ham on a rack in a shallow roasting pan. Using a sharp knife, score surface of ham with ¼-in.-deep cuts in a diamond pattern. Cover and bake 1¾ to 2¼ hours or until a thermometer reads 130°.

2. Meanwhile, place remaining ingredients in a food processor; process until blended. Remove ham from oven. Increase oven setting to 425°. Spread apricot mixture over ham.

3. Bake the ham, uncovered, 15-20 minutes longer or until a thermometer reads 140°. If desired, increase oven setting to broil; broil 2-4 minutes or until golden brown.

Cottage Potatoes

PREP: 20 MIN. • **BAKE:** 55 MIN.
MAKES: 12-14 SERVINGS

INGREDIENTS

- 12 large potatoes, peeled and diced
- 8 ounces process cheese (Velveeta), cubed
- 1 large onion, finely chopped
- 1 large green pepper, chopped
- 1 jar (2 ounces) diced pimientos, drained
- 1 slice bread, torn into crumbs
- 3 tablespoons minced fresh parsley, divided
- ½ teaspoon salt
- ½ cup milk
- ½ cup butter, melted
- 1½ cups cornflakes, crushed

DIRECTIONS

1. Place the potatoes in a saucepan or Dutch oven and cover with water. Bring to a boil; reduce heat to medium. Cover and cook for 5-7 minutes or until tender; drain. In a bowl, combine the next five ingredients. Stir in 2 tablespoons parsley and salt.
2. In a greased shallow 4-qt. baking dish, layer a third of the potatoes and a third of the cheese mixture. Repeat layers twice. Pour milk and butter over all; sprinkle with cornflake crumbs.
3. Cover and bake at 350° for 45 minutes. Uncover; bake 10-15 minutes longer or until bubbly and top is golden. Sprinkle with remaining parsley.

Sun-Dried Tomato Burgers

PREP: 30 MIN. • **GRILL:** 10 MIN. • **MAKES:** 4 SERVINGS

INGREDIENTS

- ½ cup reduced-fat sour cream
- 2 teaspoons lemon juice
- 1 garlic clove, minced
- ¼ teaspoon dried oregano
- ¼ teaspoon pepper

BURGERS
- ¼ cup oil-packed sun-dried tomatoes, chopped
- ¼ cup sun-dried tomato pesto
- 1 tablespoon salt-free Greek seasoning
- 1 pound lean ground turkey
- ¼ cup crumbled feta cheese
- 4 whole wheat hamburger buns, split
- ¼ cup chopped water-packed artichoke hearts
- ¼ cup julienned roasted sweet red peppers

DIRECTIONS

1. In a small bowl, mix the first five ingredients. Refrigerate until serving.
2. In a large bowl, combine tomatoes, pesto and Greek seasoning. Add turkey and cheese; mix lightly but thoroughly. Shape into four ½-in.-thick patties.
3. On a greased grill rack, grill burgers, covered, over medium heat, or broil 4 in. from heat 4-6 minutes on each side, until a thermometer reads 165°. Serve on buns with the sour cream mixture, artichoke hearts and peppers.

Rhubarb Strawberry Cobbler

PREP: 20 MIN. • **BAKE:** 40 MIN.
MAKES: 8 SERVINGS

INGREDIENTS

- 1⅓ cups sugar
- ⅓ cup all-purpose flour
- 4 cups sliced fresh or frozen rhubarb, thawed (½-inch pieces)
- 2 cups halved fresh strawberries
- 2 tablespoons butter, cubed

CRUST

- 2 cups all-purpose flour
- ½ teaspoon salt
- ⅔ cup canola oil
- ⅓ cup warm water
- 1 tablespoon 2% milk
- 1 tablespoon sugar
  Vanilla ice cream, optional

DIRECTIONS

1. Preheat oven to 425°. In a large bowl, mix sugar and flour. Add fruit; toss to coat. Transfer to a greased 11x7-in. baking dish. Dot with butter.

2. For crust, in a bowl, mix flour and salt. In another bowl, whisk oil and water; add to flour mixture, stirring with a fork until a dough is formed (dough will be sticky).

3. Roll the dough between two pieces of waxed paper into an 11x7-in. rectangle. Remove top piece of waxed paper; invert rectangle over filling. Gently peel off waxed paper. Brush the pastry with milk; sprinkle with sugar.

4. Bake 40-50 minutes or until golden brown. If desired, serve with ice cream.

NOTE If using frozen rhubarb, measure rhubarb while still frozen, then thaw completely. Drain in a colander, but do not press liquid out.

Lemon Chiffon Cake

PREP: 30 MIN. • **BAKE:** 50 MIN. + COOLING • **MAKES:** 16 SERVINGS

INGREDIENTS

- 7 large eggs, separated
- 2 cups all-purpose flour
- 1½ cups sugar
- 3 teaspoons baking powder
- 1 teaspoon salt
- ¾ cup water
- ½ cup canola oil
- 4 teaspoons grated lemon peel
- 2 teaspoons vanilla extract
- ½ teaspoon cream of tartar

FROSTING

- ⅓ cup butter, softened
- 3 cups confectioners' sugar
- 4½ teaspoons grated lemon peel
- ¼ cup lemon juice
  Dash salt

DIRECTIONS

1. Place egg whites in a large bowl; let stand at room temperature 30 minutes. Meanwhile, preheat oven to 325°.

2. Sift flour, sugar, baking powder and salt together twice; place in another large bowl. In a small bowl, whisk egg yolks, water, oil, lemon peel and vanilla until smooth. Add to flour mixture; beat until mixture is well blended.

3. Add cream of tartar to egg whites; with clean beaters, beat on medium speed just until stiff but not dry. Fold a fourth of the whites into batter, then fold in the remaining whites.

4. Gently spoon batter into an ungreased 10-in. tube pan. Cut through batter with a knife to remove air pockets. Bake on lowest oven rack 50-55 minutes or until top springs back when lightly touched. Immediately invert pan; cool cake completely in pan, about 1 hour.

5. Run a knife around the sides and center tube of pan. Remove cake to a serving plate.

6. In a small bowl, combine frosting ingredients; beat until smooth. Spread over cake.

Handcrafted with Love

SHARE LIFE'S SIMPLE PLEASURES.

Retread & Grow

Put a fresh spin on a classic with this repurposed planter.

WHAT YOU'LL NEED

- Motorcycle or ATV tire (see note)
- Rust-Oleum Painter's Touch 2X Ultra Cover spray paint
- Potting soil
- Flowers
- Power drill
- Heavy-duty rope

DIRECTIONS

1. Drill drainage holes in the bottom of tire if needed.

2. Spray-paint tire, building up paint in layers over the span of an hour. Let dry.

3. Plant your favorite seasonal flowers in the tire.

4. Use rope to hang planter from a tree or porch. Make sure knot is tied securely.

NOTE Used tires work better than new tires, which have a coating that can bleed through the paint. If using new tires, let dry for a couple of days after the first coat until the original tire color begins to show through, then add a fresh coat of paint.

Community Garden

Fill a pot to the brim with bean dip and plant a bunch of veggies in it for your next party. Add some breadsticks on the side, then dig in and enjoy!

WHAT YOU'LL NEED

Small clean plant pot
Plastic food storage container to fit inside plant pot (see note)
Small plate or saucer
Prepared black bean dip
Assorted fresh vegetables such as baby carrots, broccoli florets, cauliflower florets, cherry tomatoes, radishes,
Brussels sprouts
Chopped ripe olives
Fresh herbs (optional)

DIRECTIONS

1. Place the plastic food storage container inside plant pot. Fill plastic container with dip, using a spatula to smooth out the top of the dip.
2. Arrange vegetables on top of dip to create a garden patch. Gently open leaves of Brussels sprouts to resemble cabbage. If desired, poke a hole in the top of each carrot and tomato, then insert a sprig of fresh parsley, marjoram, cilantro, dill or oregano.
3. Sprinkle chopped olives around the vegetables. Place plant pot on the saucer and serve.

NOTE If your plastic food storage container sits too low in the plant pot, put some small stones in the bottom of the pot and set the container on top of them.

Sweet Stack

Turn rustic wood slices into cute mini valentines. You can also glue a magnet to the back of each for the fridge. What a fun pick-me-up!

WHAT YOU'LL NEED

Flat brush
Acrylic craft paint, purple or fuchsia
Wood slices
Paint pen (optional)
Liner brush
Chalkboard paper tag
Jute twine

DIRECTIONS

1. For each valentine, use a flat brush and regular or outdoor acrylic craft paint to paint a solid purple or fuchsia circle on front of the wood slice to within about ¼ in. of edge. Let dry.
2. Add coats as needed until paint is bright, letting dry after each coat. Paint a solid heart in center, or use a paint pen to write a message. Make a pattern of dots around the design, or add other embellishments using the paint pen or the end of a liner brush.
3. Drill a hole through each wood slice about ½ in. below the top edge. Thread a 14-in. length of jute twine through each hole, and string a chalkboard paper tag onto the twine. Secure loop with a knot.

COMMUNITY GARDEN: PRODUCED AND PHOTOGRAPHED BY MATTHEW MEAD

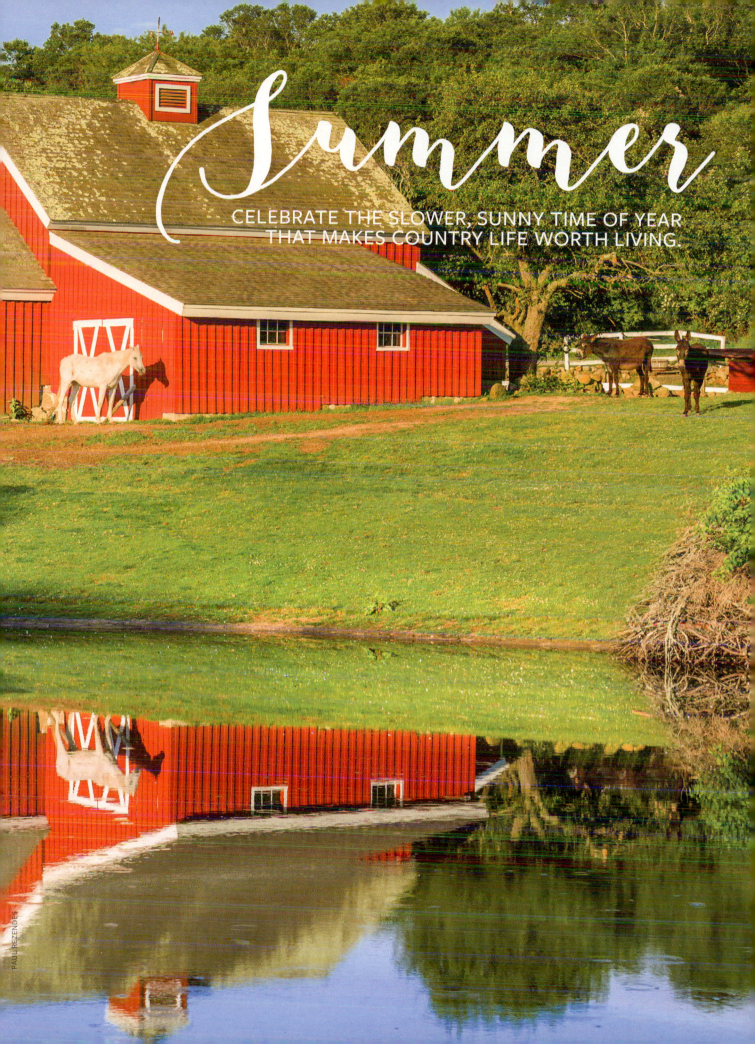

Summer

CELEBRATE THE SLOWER, SUNNY TIME OF YEAR
THAT MAKES COUNTRY LIFE WORTH LIVING.

The Good Life

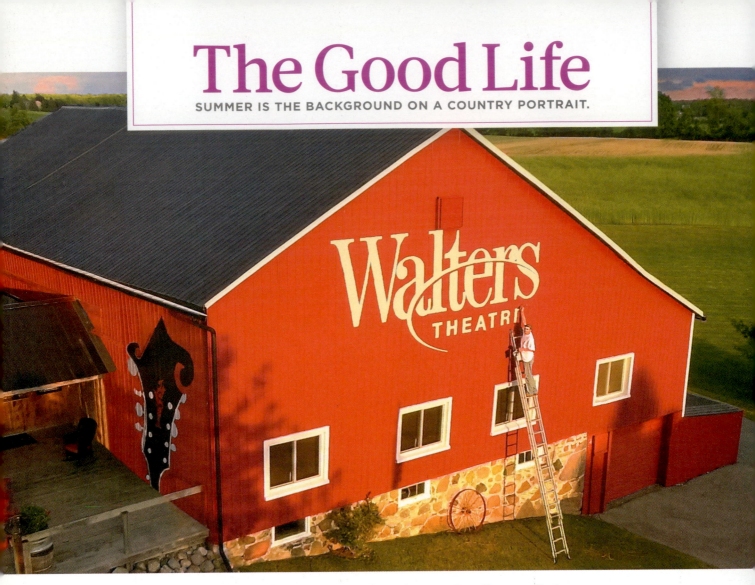

A brush with fate led to this artist's colorful country career.

The Country Is My Canvas

I was 19 in the fall of 1997 when I asked my dad if I could paint something on the hay barn. I'd always been able to get small sign-painting jobs in high school, and I wanted to work on something bigger.

With a piece of chalk in my right hand and a paper copy of the design in my left, I began freehanding marks on the weathered barn boards. Up and down the bouncy old ladder I went, checking my progress from the cow pasture, until the chalk outline perfectly matched the image on my paper. About a week later, a 20-foot Ohio State University "O" and a depiction of the Brutus Buckeye mascot decorated our old barn.

My grandfather "Pap" Hagan was so happy with the results that he snapped some photos from the seat of his John Deere Gator and took them to our local newspaper, the *Barnesville Enterprise*. The paper ran a front-page story about the barn art, and that caught the eye of a traveling spokeswoman for the state of Ohio. Next thing we knew, a man called to ask if I would be interested in painting some more barns for the Ohio bicentennial celebration in 2003!

That's when I started wondering if there was a better way to paint a barn than crawling up and down a ladder. Luckily, Dad remembered that a man known as The Barn Painter lived about 20 miles from us. Legendary Mail Pouch barn artist Harley Warrick painted or retouched more than 20,000 barns during his 55-year career. And after a few phone calls, the 74-year-old welcomed me to his shop.

Harley was well into retirement at that point, but he still painted and sold mailboxes and birdhouses. He happily showed me his scaffolding rig and sternly explained, "You'll need this right here. This setup is a block and tackle. It did well for me for 45 years." He told me what to buy, how to fabricate it, what lengths of ropes to buy, and how to quickly tie them.

I stopped by many times after that. Harley was a pleasant fellow who loved to talk politics and share adventures from his Mail Pouch days. Harley died in 2000 at age 76, and I'll be forever grateful for his gracious and generous help. I still use the walking plank he gave me.

In 1998, I started painting an Ohio bicentennial logo on barns in each of Ohio's 88 counties. Over the next five years, the paintings often became local events. I found myself speaking at schools and on TV. People came with lawn chairs and picnics to watch the red, white and blue "Ohio" take shape, and sometimes applause would even break out when I finished the last brushstroke.

The barns became a centerpiece of the celebration and even won an award for creative advertising. Most of those 88 barns are still standing, and people still enjoy visiting them on driving tours.

Since I finished that project in 2003, I have painted hundreds of other structures across the U.S. and Canada. When customers ask for a quote, I ask them to send me quality photos of the structure. Then I use Adobe Photoshop to draw possible designs on the photos so customers can see exactly how the paintings would look. In addition to barns, I've painted silos, grain elevators, football fields and rooftops.

Sometimes a client wants the painting to look old and weathered. I used that style inside a pro golfer's home and on a vintage Coca-Cola sign in Illinois.

To improve my speed and safety on the job, I'm always inventing tools or crafting hardware, such as oversized protractors, marking extensions or special magnets for metal-sided buildings. I now draw the outline with black and white grease pencils instead of chalk, and I graduated from ropes to aluminum scaffolding that can move up and down with the aid of an electric drill. The scaffolding gives me great freedom of movement and makes me feel safe.

My jobs aren't always near paint stores, restaurants and hotels, so I try to be as self-sufficient as possible.

Scott Hagan (far left, above left, and immediate right) painted an Ohio State tribute on his dad's hay barn (below) that started him on a lifetime career.

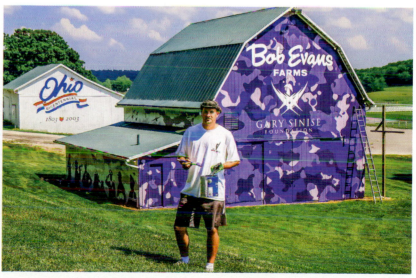

Scott was asked to paint 88 barns for Ohio's bicentennial. Since then, he's painted hundreds of other barns and structures across the U.S. and Canada.

I haul all the ladders and scaffolding on my truck's heavy-duty ladder racks, and I tow a toy hauler travel trailer that's a camper and storage for my pressure washer, paint sprayer, torpedo heater, generator and bulk paints. I basically camp at the site until the work is done. Some jobs use less than a gallon of paint; others can take 45 gallons if the customer wants several sides painted. I usually carry all the primary colors and mix them on site to create all the custom colors I need.

Besides setting up the scaffolding, weather is my biggest challenge. In the early years, rain showers would catch me off guard and ruin hours of work. Today, scanning the weather radar on my smartphone usually helps me stay ahead of the rain, but I still have to keep an eye on the sky in areas with no cell service. I quickly learned not to bother with rain tarps. They turn into wildly flapping sails under the slightest breeze. I'm sorry to say that wind is my sworn enemy at any temperature.

Seeing our country is one of the biggest perks of my profession. I'd like to paint at least one barn in all 50 states—and I'm getting there. Sometimes my family comes along to make it a bit of a vacation. I'm looking forward to the day when they also can help with the painting!

I hope you can tell that I really enjoy what I do. After nearly 20 years of painting, I give thanks to my mother for showing me how to draw, to my father for teaching me how to work, to my grandfather for believing in me and sharing that first barn picture, and to the state of Ohio for taking a big chance on a 20-year-old kid. Most of all, thanks be to God. I can't wait to see where He takes me next!

**Scott Hagan
Jerusalem, Ohio**

Cherry Surprise

There's a funny story behind my mother's pickled cherry tomatoes.

Our soil in Virginia was very poor—all red clay—so when a local farmer offered my father all the composted manure he could haul away, Dad jumped at the chance. He took the backseats out of the car, lined everything with plastic, and came home with three big trash cans full of manure, which he spread on the vegetable garden.

Turns out, it wasn't very well composted. Oh, how the yard stank! We were so glad when winter set in and froze the ground hard. The next spring, we turned the soil and planted a typical suburban vegetable garden: corn, squash and peas. That summer, an astonishing number of cherry tomatoes popped up everywhere in the garden. But we hadn't planted them. It seems that our free compost came with bonus seeds!

We ate tomatoes all summer. And then pickled tomatoes for the rest of the year.

Helen Nelander
Boulder Creek, CA

"Our grandson Noah and our miniature Hereford love playing on summer days,"
MARCELLA KAHN
PLAINVIEW, MINNESOTA

"I took this photo while my husband, Cody, and I were on a run. This pasture is on a street near our house where we have beautiful scenery to look at every day."
APRIL POWELL
CRAWFORDVILLE, GEORGIA

"This is Jayda, a little friend and daughter of our pastor. Here she is in her family's chicken coop, using an egg carton to get those fresh ones safely back to the house. She must have a real way with those chickens!"
PATRICIA HAIGHT
GILBOA, NEW YORK

My Outside Office

For 15 years, I dressed up in suits and high heels and headed off to work. I took pride in my high-pressure job as an administrator of an assisted living center. Offering the best care to residents, juggling state regulations and providing delicious, healthy meals was a challenge I looked forward to each day.

I would probably still be there if a new company hadn't bought out our chain and decided to bring in its own administrators. When I was asked to pack up my things, it felt like the worst day of my life. Our residents were like family to me.

After a few months of sadness, I woke up on a sunny morning and walked onto our 20-acre farm. The horses were grazing in the meadows and the chickens were scratching in the dirt. Birds sang all around, and squirrels hurried from one pecan tree to another. All of the beauty and tranquility made me stop and realize I should enjoy this simple life. My husband, Andy, and I had bought this little farm 20 years before, but I was so caught up in my career that I could not appreciate it.

I began to take more interest in our horses. They each have a unique personality, and spending time with them gave me joy. So we went to an auction and bought three miniature horses. I helped Andy build a barn for the minis and decorated it with photos, colorful feed buckets and personalized tack. Next we put up a board fence, which gave the new horses a pasture to graze and roam.

Then we decided to add to our chicken population, so we began researching all kinds of bird breeds. Each day I would grab my basket and run down to the chicken coops, eager to see how many colored eggs I would get.

I found a new sense of energy and jumped out of bed each morning. Instead of my usual routine—fixing my hair, getting dressed up, and sporting those uncomfortable high heels—I now pulled on jeans and work boots.

Things were going so well that we decided to plant a huge garden. The fresh veggies were delicious, and we started eating healthier. I learned to can and filled the freezer with corn, butterbeans and squash.

Our house began to look like a grocery store, so we built a cannery building with a root cellar. Now we have the perfect place to process and store all our produce. Next year, I plan to sell eggs and veggies at the local farmers market to bring in a little income.

My life has changed drastically. I now have a spring in my step, even though I am working harder than ever. We have many more plans to make our hobby farm one of a kind, and it is a delight to sit down and plan our dreams.

For anyone who is beginning to feel burned out, I suggest starting a little farm. It doesn't matter how big it is, as long as it is yours—and you can make it any way you want.

I know I wouldn't change back into my suits and high heels for all the money in the world.

Jill Wilmoth
Scottsburg, Virginia

Jill's new office is 20 acres of pasture. From horses to hens, Jill practices leading with one of her mini horses (right) and collects eggs from the chicken coops (far right).

"On a foggy morning drive near Gettysburg National Military Park, I couldn't help but think of the soldiers who fought there."
SUSAN GROVE
GETTYSBURG, PENNSYLVANIA

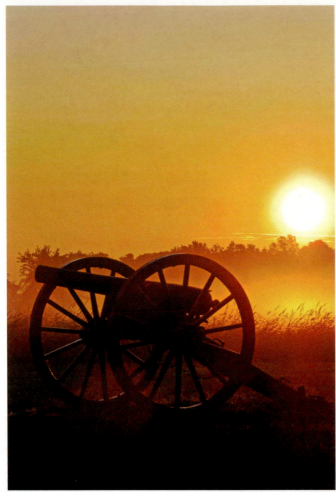

"A friend and I were on the hunt for a moose to photograph in Grand Teton National Park. After fruitless searching, this fellow appeared."
KATHERINE PLESSNER
VERONA, NORTH DAKOTA

Nature's Playground

I was sure my parents had forgotten my 10th birthday. After a day of hiking the canyons and playing in the river, however, they surprised me with presents and a "cake" of mini doughnuts.

The 100th birthday of our National Park Service reminded me of that birthday at Zion and all the other times my parents took us on such adventures. In my 28 years, I've visited 29 national parks and countless other historic sites.

My grandparents started this tradition when they drove through 49 states, taking my dad and his brothers camping. Our bedtime stories were laden with mischievous tales of those childhood trips. Dad gave us kids the chance to see his stories come alive while creating our own tales to tell.

The Knodel family, with two girls the same ages as my brother and me, were a vital part of our travels. The four of us became Junior Rangers at almost every park we visited.

Our imaginations ran wild in nature's playground. On the lava formations at Craters of the Moon in Idaho, we became space explorers. The Badlands in the Dakotas were our castles, with dragons lurking around every corner. We were pioneers on the prairie and Indians on the hunt for buffalo.

The adventures continue today. Last summer, my mom and I went to Acadia National Park in Maine. We marveled at mighty ocean waves crashing on the rocks, felt the sea breeze on our cheeks, and curled our toes in wet sand. As we listened to water lapping against rocks, memories of family camping trips came flooding back. Traditions passed on from my grandparents and parents are a part of me, and I am grateful for that.

I can hardly wait to return to the national parks of my childhood and experience them as an adult. There is nothing in the world like falling asleep to the rhythm of chirping crickets and waking up to the stillness of the woods. Nature was created for our enjoyment, and our national parks preserve this gift for each generation. Whether you are turning 10 or 100, you couldn't receive a more lasting birthday gift than experiencing the beauty of our national parks.

Melissa Hansen
Milwaukee, Wisconsin

A Walk in the Country

During every nature walk, I acquire a new treasure that calms my mind. I could never list all the things I've learned from the colors, aromas and feelings that overtake my senses in the great outdoors.

It isn't peaceful in the country; there is constant activity going on. It's loud and busy as life strives to survive. But my own pressures seem to shrink in comparison. I have found hiking up in the mountains to be a bit easier than on level ground because there are plenty of landmarks to guide me back. I'll never forget the time an elk stalked out from the swaying pines and fir trees. He regally lifted his head after drinking water, and his breath streamed around his furry face as he snorted into the air.

I call hiking on the level ground "trekking," which I adore, especially if it involves water. I will always take the time to take off my shoes and socks and wade into a stream. I like the feeling of little perch nibbling on my ankles.

And I consider walking down a country road in Texas as much of a hike, or trek, as anything else.

Once I was going along with my dog, Tator, who is a mix of the common breeds: dumb and lovey. We were enjoying the katydids buzzing in the mesquites and the sunflowers bowing to us along the wire fences. We came into an open farmyard with two bulls chomping on the grass. My silly dog got excited, barking to say hello.

The older bull continued eating without batting an ear. So my dog decided to greet the younger one with the same gusto, and that did not go so well. The indignant bull stomped, and Tator tucked tail and ran toward me. That day our walk was cut short, but we still had a great time.

I have never gotten lost in the country. I do, however, get lost in civilization and the overwhelming stress about things that seem so important. I also lose my perspective and my inner self, and that is probably a whole lot worse.

When I take the time—and it's never wasted—to walk along in a natural place, I am found again.

Leonora Raye
Lockhart, Texas

"Our granddaughter Anna loves jumping across hay bales when she comes up from South Carolina to visit her Uncle Richard's farm. She might be a city girl, but there's country in her heart."
MARYANNE SETTLE
NEWARK VALLEY, NEW YORK

Take time to soak in all the glory that a summer in the country has to offer.

COUNTER CLOCKWISE FROM THE TOP:

"We're proud of our country and the crops growing in the summer sun, and we sure are proud of that tractor. Our Fourth of July festivities include a celebration of the all-American farmer."
Kris Klingaman
FAIRBANK, IOWA

"Nothing beats summertime in the country. My love of it has grown watching my sweet boy enjoy it over these past two years. This captures him taking it all in."
Felicia Frazier
MURFREESBORO, TENNESSEE

"A farmer works sunrise to sunset, and this picture of my husband, Mike, plowing at dusk is a reminder of the hard work that goes into our happy lives."
Tammy Otremba
PIERZ, MINNESOTA

"Sunshine, green grass and cows. That's summer at LouAllen Farms. Hot weather makes for long days, but there's no beating the fun that follows all those hours in the fields."
Hollie LouAllen
MOULTON, ALABAMA

Summer Scrapbook

SOAK IN ALL THAT THE COUNTRY HAS TO OFFER THIS SEASON.

Enjoy the sweet rewards of summer's labor across this big blooming country.

"The sun shining behind a Colonial flag made the past very present to me."
DANNY REDD
GALAX, VIRGINIA

"My son, Cody, admires his great-grandpappy's tractor."
KATRINA DREW
YEMASSEE, SOUTH CAROLINA

"We drove across the country last summer and marveled at the diversity of gorgeous scenery, like this Idaho farm field."
MIKE CONTOS
NAPLES, NEW YORK

"Flocks of bushtits visit our property year-round. Although they rarely get close enough for a photo, I got lucky with this one."
JOAN SPARKS
CUPERTINO, CALIFORNIA

"I saw these two children at play while their father loaded the truck in Holmes County, Ohio. Even at a young age, this girl knows who is the boss!"
MARY LOU SMITH
BETHEL PARK, PENNSYLVANIA

The Short family's garden shed near Pittsfield, Maine, is surrounded by a rainbow of blooming perennials.
PHOTO BY TERRY WILD STOCK

Country kids remind us of carefree living, the glories of the season and those warm summer days gone by.

Country girl Stella and her buddy are having a grand adventure in the back of this old truck.
PHOTO BY LONDIE GARCIA PADELSKY
SAN LUIS OBISPO, CALIFORNIA

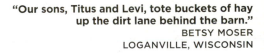

"Our sons, Titus and Levi, tote buckets of hay up the dirt lane behind the barn."
BETSY MOSER
LOGANVILLE, WISCONSIN

"My granddaughter Cheyenne, then 6, won a county fair blue ribbon for her Hereford calf. The animal loves Cheyenne and even head-butts anyone who tries to play with her."
DEBBIE BRIDGES
SHELBY, NORTH CAROLINA

"We live on a dairy farm in western Chester County. Our son, Dustin, age 3, loves to run and play all over the farm, and the kittens are his favorite playmates."
ANDREA SMOKER
PARKESBURG, PENNSYLVANIA

"There was a lot of congestion at the feeders, but this female ruby-throated hummingbird waited on a black-eyed Susan until the drama at the 'water cooler' was over."
JON MONTGOMERY
DU QUOIN, ILLINOIS

"This escaped chicken enjoyed brunch in the garden before we rounded her up."
HANNAH RING
CONNEAUT, OHIO

"I found a black bear snacking on mountain ash berries in Grand Teton National Park."
BONNIE BOWNE
FORT COLLINS, COLORADO

"A variegated fritillary butterfly paused to savor some nectar from a lovely mist flower. I came across the fluttery little friend on planting day, when we sowed the fields in late spring."
JEAN WATSON
UNIONTOWN, ALABAMA

"Two American goldfinches made themselves at home at my bird feeder a few summers ago. I loved their big personalities."
TRISH NEVAN
ASTORIA, OREGON

A country road winds through
Sangerville, Virginia.
PHOTO BY PAT &
CHUCK BLACKLEY

Summer's invitation to explore the country is open to all every hour of every glorious day.

"I climbed a silo at sunrise to catch this moody shot of morning mist on the cropland (above) and (right) the sun rising behind Star, our family horse."
HANNAH RING
CONNEAUT, OHIO

Mother Nature colors the world with her brightest and finest creations. Remember to stop and appreciate her lovely efforts.

The flag waits for a breeze on a warm July morning.
PHOTO BY PATTI MCCONVILLE/ ALAMY STOCK PHOTO

"One Saturday morning, my husband and I noticed a ruby-throated hummingbird relishing the rain. These birds are usually in motion, so it was a peaceful sight to see this one perched contentedly, neck stretched with its head to the sky, truly enjoying the moment."
MARY MEYER
EYOTA, MINNESOTA

"Even from the height of a helicopter, the majesty of Mount Rushmore inspires deep feelings of patriotism."
RON LINTON
RAPID CITY, SOUTH DAKOTA

"Ryan, our granddaughter, was not about to share her first taste of watermelon!"
LAREEN LITTLEWOOD
MIDVALE, UTAH

"My sultan bantams get a bright-eyed, curious expression when any critter walks by. They're truly backyard clowns."
DAWN KOPP
DRYDEN, MICHIGAN

"On vacation in Great Smoky Mountains National Park, we drove up to Clingmans Dome, the highest point in the park, and watched this most amazing sunset."
PHILIP STEURY
AUBURN, INDIANA

"These farmers were demonstrating old-time wheat threshing practices in Lancaster County."
DIANE ANDRE
BOYERTOWN,
PENNSYLVANIA

The front porch of a cottage in Ellisport, Washington, invites passers-by to sit for a spell.
PHOTO BY TERRY DONNELLY

"A farmer outside town showed his patriotism by draping a flag on a weathered work cart."
LINDA TODD-LIMON
JULIAN, CALIFORNIA

"Kaleb shows his little cousin William the ropes at the rodeo while wearing grandpa-made chaps."
PATRICIA BIGALK
WHITE BEAR LAKE, MINNESOTA

Holstein dairy cows graze and gaze at the Blue Ridge Mountains near Dayton, Ohio.
PHOTO BY PAT & CHUCK BLACKLEY

Heart & Soul

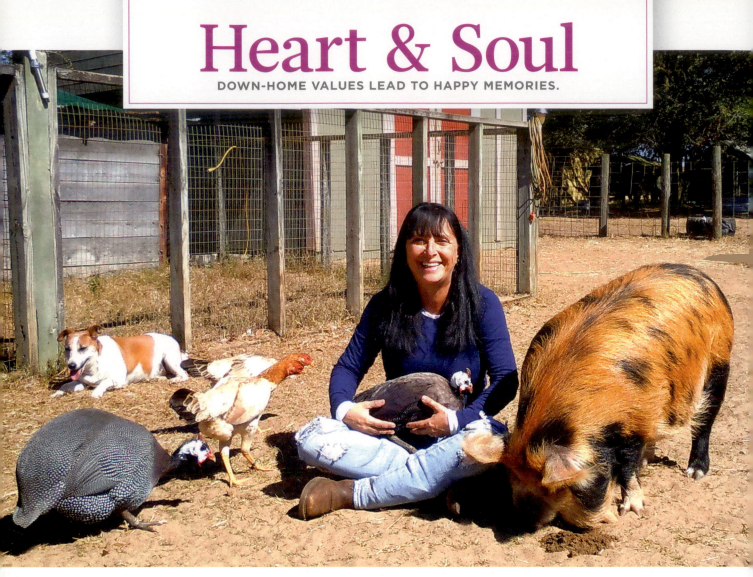

She found her purpose in life—saving abused, neglected and unwanted farm animals.

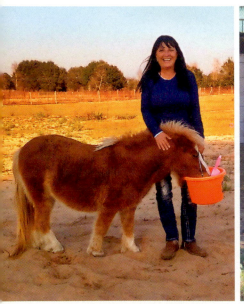

She Won Country Woman of the Year

I would like to nominate my wife of 24 years, Ann-Marie Roberts, as *Country Woman* magazine's Country Woman of the Year! Raised in New York City and working in the fashion industry, she never got her hands dirty. Then, eight years ago, I wanted to reconnect to my country roots, but how would I inspire the same feeling in, well, a try city woman?

I considered her natural passion for children and babies, so I brought her a 2-month-old potbellied pig. AnnMarie instantly bonded with Penelope, and soon we added two puppies to our family.

Within four months, she'd rescued her first animal, another potbellied pig that quickly became more than its owners—college students—could handle. It needed a place where it could be a pig, not a party favor.

AnnMarie knew she'd found her purpose in life: to rescue abused, neglected and unwanted farm animals. Now we needed a place where she could do that. We bought a 5-acre property on Sugarloaf Mountain in Clermont, Florida, and started a farm.

That's when she became a true country woman, facing challenges with grace and limitless energy.

Not long after we moved, the big recession hit. Then flooding in central Florida caused many to lose their homes. Requests for us to take in more animals were overwhelming, but AnnMarie didn't flinch for a moment. She fought to find homes for every one. If she couldn't find a new home, that critter came to live with us.

Currently, we have about 300 animals. Some of them are blind, deaf, disabled, survivors of severe abuse or simply unwanted. But here, AnnMarie gives them a safe place to rest their heads and a loving forever home. She is the sole caretaker for this entire farm of ours.

From sunrise to sunset, and often long into the night, she cleans, feeds and cares for every single animal. For that, they absolutely adore her.

Our neighbors just love AnnMarie, and they also appreciate that if they call with an emergency, she'll gladly offer assistance. AnnMarie has taken her experience of delivering baby animals to other farms, sometimes saving a newborn by getting its breath started. She has built quite the reputation as a knowledgeable animal caregiver.

Last year she decided she wanted to do more, so she had our farm certified as a nonprofit animal rescue. This will allow her to add more pens and housing, plus a medical facility for providing even better treatment to critical-care animals.

She would love to educate people about the huge responsibility involved in owning a pet and encourage them to thoroughly research and plan before making a decision to buy or adopt.

My wife has been described as a ball of energy. A few times, she's gone so fast, she's found herself in a tricky situation—like the time she trapped herself in the chicken pen. As she was racing by, she noticed that it needed to be cleaned, so she went inside to do just that. She also shut the door to keep the chicks from getting out. Only then did she realize that when I built the coop, I designed the door in a way that locked her in. Luckily, I soon found her—she was sitting in the middle of the coop with 10 chicks nestled in her lap.

AnnMarie has the biggest, kindest heart. Her dedication to her work and passion for her family and animals has no bounds. Plus, she always makes sure I have plenty of homemade sweet tea. Now that's a country woman!

I feel if anyone deserves to be called a country hero, it's my wife. But even if she doesn't win this contest, AnnMarie will always be my country woman, my love and my hero.

Keith Roberts
Clermont, Florida

Keith (below) nominated his wife AnnMarie (opposite and right) as Country Woman of the Year. Her work saving animals and housing them on the family farm won her the 2016 tile.

Shining for Jesus

Slowly filing into the auditorium each morning, we sang this lovely verse: "Come to Bible school, be on time each day, here we learn to shine for Jesus, in our work and play."

Back in the 1950s, vacation Bible school at Tangent Mennonite Church in Tangent, Oregon, was something we looked forward to eagerly each year. Classes were held every summer from 9 a.m. to noon, five days a week for two weeks. Children came from all over the community. It was fun to be together.

I was too young to realize or to appreciate the sacrifices our parents made to send us to Bible school. For my mother, it involved rising early to run our dirty clothes through the wringer washer and hang them on an outdoor line, picking produce in the garden, cooking a substantial breakfast for our family of eight children, getting us ready to leave on time and picking up neighbor children en route. On top of all that, she taught a class.

We loved the prizes that came our way when we brought in a new student or memorized a designated portion of scripture. The pennies, nickels and dimes we donated went to China for Bibles or to Africa to feed orphans, giving us a feeling of satisfaction in helping to meet some church and world needs.

On the last day, we were treated to ice cream bars and gifts from our teachers. And that evening, we gave a program for our parents to share what we had learned—it evoked excitement, as well as trepidation, among the students.

My favorite memory is a lesson I learned when I was in eighth grade. Our teacher challenged the class to go the second mile and do more than you are asked,

as in the Bible. The next day, we gave a report on what we had done. Sandy's mother asked her to clear the table, so she swept the floor, too. Norman not only mowed the lawn but also weeded the flower bed.

Kay didn't just wash the dishes as asked; she also dried them and put them in the cupboard. Addison lived on a dairy farm and informed us that when his dad sent him to bring the cows in for milking, he brought the calves in as well. Mother asked me to set the table, which I did, and then I washed the dishes after dinner.

When I was 14 years old, I got roped into teaching a kindergarten class. I had no teaching experience, but I enjoyed it. My parents gave me time off from chores one afternoon so I could make an attendance chart out of construction paper. I always marveled at how they supported me in doing such a thing at a young age. We shined for Jesus in those days, for Bible school was work and play.

Eunice Mast
Chewelah, Washington

Eunice, 14, got the afternoon off from farm chores to make an attendance chart for her class (at right).

The pigs wreaked havoc in Kristin's front yard.

Mending Fences

The pancakes were on the table, and our little family of three was about to dive into breakfast. As I poured maple syrup over my stack, our 2-year-old daughter, Jean, leapt from her chair.

"Mama, Mama ... Pigs!" she yelled, making oinking noises in her little girl's voice. She pointed out the window to our wooded backyard.

Now I leapt from my chair, slamming down my fork in anger, and grabbed the truck keys.

"Wait for me," my husband, Mark, bellowed as he wrestled with his boots and jumped up to follow me out the door.

"Stay on the porch," I told Jean, as Mark and I hopped in the pickup and drove it recklessly around the yard. We honked and screamed as we chased the pigs off our property for what must have been the 10th time that summer.

Our neighbors had rented a small pigpen to some old family friends so they could keep pigs. The friends didn't do a good job with the upkeep of the pen, so the pigs kept escaping and vandalizing not only our garden and yard but also our neighbors'. We called the owners of the pigs several times, but the man was old, and it was hard for him to get out to the pigpen to make repairs. We called the police but were told nothing could be done.

It was a frustrating situation for all of us who lived on that dirt road.

"That's it! I've had enough!" I said. "I'm heading right over there to come up with a plan to make this craziness end."

Mark, Jean and I drove to Angie's and William's place. They were in the middle of breakfast when we knocked on their screen door.

"Come on in," William called out.
"The pigs are out again," I huffed.

William got up from his breakfast and said, "I've had just about enough of them. I reckon it's time to get out the shotguns and take care of all this nonsense ourselves."

"No!" cried Zora, the couple's 6-year-old daughter. "It's not the pigs' fault. Can't we just fix the pen so they don't escape anymore?"

Silence. We had been so full of finger-pointing and anger that we had all forgotten it was within our power to fix the problem with a little sweat and some human kindness.

The anger boiling inside me slowed to a simmer, and then it was gone. I knelt down to talk to her.

"Zora, we will fix the pen. Thank you for reminding us that violence is not a solution." She beamed.

Later that day, we went down to the pen and repaired the broken gate. It took several hours of our time and several dollars of our hard-earned money, but the day was beautiful and the kids frolicked in the nearby hayfield.

We never told the owner of the pigs what we had done, but a few months later, the ailing old man found himself in better health. He stopped by to apologize for the chaos his pigs caused.

Later that evening, we invited the neighbors over for dinner and again thanked Zora for coming up with a simple solution to the pig problem.

The kids laughed as we feasted and celebrated an act of compassion. Our bellies were full, and so were our hearts.

Kristin Baczynski
Duck River, Tennessee

Make Do With What You Got

My husband, Norman, and I bought an 1837 schoolhouse in 2009 after admiring it for 25 years. It transported us back to the days when Sewickley Township was a bustling place.

Along the curve at the bottom of the hollow, a gristmill used water from the nearby creek to grind grain, and a train station sheltered travelers on their journeys. A dirt road carried horse and buggy riders past our one-room schoolhouse.

The stone foundation, slate roof, slender cream windows and bell tower perched atop the structure all had seen better days. As carpenters by trade, we did not waste any time and began restoring it.

The repairs took us a few years, and we hit an unexpected obstacle. As we approached the south wall, we heard a loud buzzing and saw a few friendly flybys. Upon closer investigation, we discovered a colony of honeybees. Looking at the size of it, these girls had been in the wall for a very long time.

Being avid gardeners, we did not want to kill the bees, but we had no idea where to begin. To find a person to move them and place them in a hive is not easy or inexpensive, so we worked around the bees for about a year. They brought back a flood of warm memories of my great-grandfather, Michael Dudik, tending to his flowers, vegetables and bees. "You make do with what you got," he would say in his thick Slovak accent.

With that advice in mind, the decision to keep the bees was easy. We were lucky to find a friendly local beekeeper, Mr. Faucet, who was kind enough to come to our property and place the honeybees in a brood box. With support and help from the community, we were able to establish the hive that we now fondly refer to as our "schoolgirls."

Before we knew it, we were in love with the wonderful world of honeybees. And Norman started building hives for other beekeepers to fund finishing the schoolhouse.

We thought beekeeping would be a great business, so we took honey to a local Italian club as a test. I had to make three trips home for more jars!

Many local businesses stocked our honey to help us get started. I picked the name Crimson Creek Apiaries because the maples along the water in the fall turn bright red.

Our business of honey production and pollination is going strong, and it is now our full-time job. We sell products at local festivals, make wedding favors and plan to open up a honey store.

If you need to relocate a swarm, call "Swarmin' Norman." His pals used to call him Stormin' Norman, but they changed the nickname after they saw him working with bees.

We offer field trips for kids at the schoolhouse and presentations at garden clubs and churches. It's so rewarding to share our knowledge about beekeeping and the value of making do with what you got!

Linda Lachimia
Irwin, Pennsylvania

Bees (above) were a delightful, although unexpected, surprise for Linda and Norman Lachimia, who eventually turned an old schoolhouse (right) into an education center for aspiring bee keepers.

Swarmin' Norman presents "Beeing One With Nature" during a field trip. Below, different nectars create different honey colors. Norman collected one swarm from the cherry tree and moved the bees to his handmade hive boxes.

Restoring an old schoolhouse brought a swarm of "schoolgirls" and a lot of lessons learned.

Road-Tripping With Mom

I once asked my 77-year-old mother, Lois, to accompany me a road trip through northern New England. We would be traveling to see my daughter, Caitlin, who was working in New Hampshire. The trip took us from western Massachusetts through Vermont and to the mountain ranges of New Hampshire.

Once we hit the road, our discussions touched on family eccentricities, childhood memories and current events. Every so often our conversation slowed as we took in the the beauty only a leisurely summer drive through New England can offer.

Before long we arrived in Caitlin's town, Franconia. Mom and I took a side trip to Littleton, explored the charming downtown area and "played" the artsy pianos on the sidewalks. We stopped on Main Street at Chutters, home of the world's longest candy counter, where colorful glass jars boasted more than 500 types of tempting treats. We felt like kids again!

With sweets in hand, we walked to the Riverwalk Covered Bridge to watch the exuberant waters of the Ammonoosuc River flowing just below. After a brief time we headed back to Main Street's antique shops, clothing stores, art galleries and gift shops, all begging for our browsing attention.

The next morning, just before our "breakfeast" at Polly's Pancake Parlor in Franconia, my mother was greeted by a black bear sitting on the steep, grassy slope just outside my daughter's bedroom window.

Mom was fearfully unenthusiastic about the visitor, but Caitlin assured her that the bear would wander back to its home before we left.

After breakfast, Mom and I bid farewell to Caitlin and headed to the Cannon Mountain Aerial Tramway in Franconia Notch State Park. As we ascended in the tram, dozens of mountaintops seemed to ripple endlessly over miles of green landscape. Once on top, we took a narrow and at times slippery trail bound for the observation deck.

From the tram we passed by the decrepit remains of the Old Man of the Mountain's face, an ancient rock formation that looked like a man's profile before it collapsed. Arriving at the Flume, we took photos of the thundering waters, breathing in the glorious scent of fresh hemlock greens as we alternately hiked and rested along the wooden walkways and hilly trails.

After we conquered a more challenging part of the trail, I snapped a photo of Mom—hunched over but still managing to smile for the camera. I texted the photo to my sisters with the caption "My daughter's trying to kill me at the Flume." They loved it, and so did Mom. What a trooper! The hike may have challenged her athletic prowess, but the rewards for this observant bird- and plant-lover far outweighed any exhaustion.

By 7 p.m. that day, we were home, retracing our steps with my dad and my husband. The next morning, as I stood in the kitchen waiting for the troops to assemble for breakfast, Mom slowly walked by me, stopped and gently grabbed me around the waist, laying her head lovingly on my shoulder.

Road-tripping with my mom was two days full of experiences that culminated in a hug that told the entire story.

Kathy Gates Milewski
Chewelah, Washington

Grandpa Lupkes (right) laid the barn's brick walls with the help of his sons and some good friends.

Built to Last...and Last

My husband, Jim, and I live on his grandparents' farm. Grandpa George Sr. and Grandma Jennie moved here from Iowa with 11 children in 1928 and had one more child here. Jim's dad, Ole, was the second-oldest son.

After helping to build a brick library in a nearby town, Grandpa decided to replace the farm's original barn with a new brick one. He designed it himself and built it with the help of his five sons and a few friends. They used field rock picked from the farm to build a foundation, and then they poured a concrete floor over that. They mixed their own mortar and laid brick walls 9 feet high. The barn is 33x56 feet, so it took a lot of bricks and hard work.

The gable ends of the hayloft are made of wood; one end has a large door for loading hay into the loft. Each end also has a smaller door to pitch the hay out. Grandpa topped off the roof with a big cupola holding up a weather vane with a glass ball and cow on it.

Inside, the barn had stanchions for 12 milk cows, a calf pen, a bull pen and a calving pen. All the pens were made of steel pipe set in the concrete floor. To say that Grandpa built a very solid barn is quite an understatement.

We put on a new green metal roof 13 years ago, and that's the only thing we've had to replace in 68 years. We still use the barn for beef cattle and usually keep about 10 cows. We put the calves in the calf pen after they're weaned.

We feed out the yearlings on the side of the barn where the stanchions used to be. Grandpa's steel pipes are still solidly sunk into the concrete, so the yearlings eat hay through the old stanchion pipes as if they were a hay feeder.

The barn has served its family well, and in many ways. There was never a dull moment with 12 brothers and sisters feeding and milking together. Like kids have for five generations now, they built forts in the haymow, played with kittens and swung on the big rope that opened and closed the haymow door. They were pirates, cowboys and circus performers, as well as young farmers.

Grandpa's barn has been a place for good times, a place to learn and a place for kids to grow up into hardworking, efficient, dependable adults. We feel very honored and fortunate to live here.

Luella Lupkes
Wheaton, Minnesota

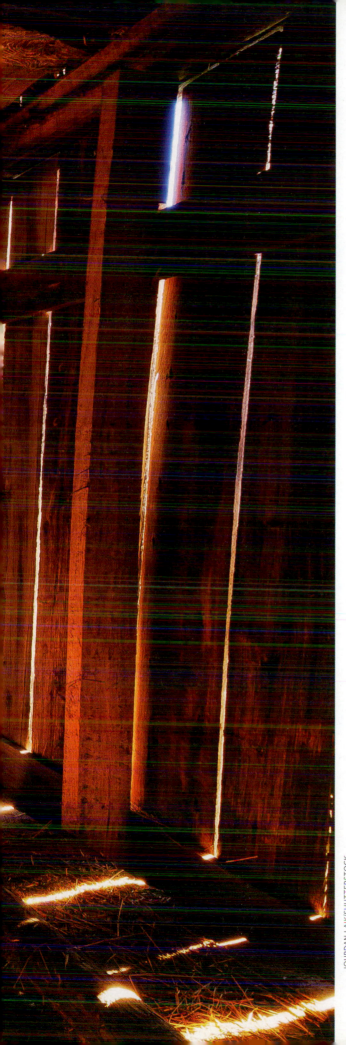

A Farm Kid's Sanctuary

The little white barn door creaks open, revealing thousands of dust fairies dancing on a sunlit stage. I step into the barn and join shadows formed by mows of hay and cluttered groups of machinery. The barn floor lies in stillness before me like a giant treasure chest waiting to be opened by my young, adventurous soul.

The aroma of fresh hay filters down from neatly stacked bales, mixing itself with the dusty odor of scraggly meadow grass still unused after a year of patient waiting. Cattle and fermenting silage nearby add their scents to create a barn recipe loved by generations of farmers and their children.

My footsteps are soft and quiet. I walk on a thick carpet of hay stems and leaves. Frightened kittens hide themselves, too shy to be in my company. A golden mound of wheat partially covers the floor. I take two handfuls of grain and let them fall through my fingers like sparkling raindrops. I pop a few grains into my mouth and begin to chew. Soon the golden morsels become a wheat gum that feels gushy on my tongue.

Chewing my homemade treat, I make my way past Gramps' precious Ford Jubilee and the well-used hay wagon, parked a little too crooked for Dad's liking. The green of the John Deere 4020 draws me close, and I strain my growing muscles to pull myself up to the controls. I'm at home in the padded yellow seat and sit a little taller as I daydream about the day when tractor duty will be included in my farm chores.

After finishing the imaginary fieldwork, I scramble up the wooden ladder to the hayloft, careful to avoid the splintery rails, loose rungs and cobwebs. I jump from towers of carefully stacked hay, which will be greatly appreciated when the winter winds are howling, but I steer clear of the treacherous hay hole. Still, I can't resist pushing some loose hay down on unsuspecting cows below.

Suddenly, I hear scratching and pawing outside. The small barn door creaks open, and in bursts our dog, Rusty. He clambers up over the bales and joins me in search of a soft bed of loose hay. I lie down with my pal at my side and stare up at the huge wooden beams and barn rafters. My mind fills with images of long ago when strong, calloused hands and sweaty bodies worked together to build this old barn. Their purpose then was far different from mine on this lazy summer day.

Soon my dreams are interrupted by the familiar call of "milking time." I race Rusty from bale to bale down to the floor. I unroll my pant cuffs to let the dust and hay go free. The little barn door creaks shut, and the dust fairies must continue their dance in darkness, until I return another day.

Jane L. Horning
Washington Boro, Pennsylvania

The Core of a Grocery Store

Bringing back memories one apple at a time.

I loved visiting my grandparents' small country grocery store. At one time, the wood building had been painted red, but I remember it being faded and in need of new paint. It wasn't falling down, but it had a slight lean.

The front door had a large glass window, and the words "Colonial Bread" were painted on the screen door in yellow. The floor creaked under your feet as you walked in. To the left was the candy counter, which seemed about a mile long, at least when I was young. Beyond that was the service counter with the big cash register on it.

On your right was the pot-bellied coal stove that heated the entire building. An odd assortment of seats, consisting of some empty wooden Coca-Cola crates, a large block of wood, and a couple of dilapidated chairs, made a semicircle around the back of the stove. The produce was just past this half-circle. In the fall, overflowing bushels of red and green apples sat front and center so customers would be sure to see them.

Often, it was the men who came into the store with the shopping lists. While Granddaddy Young filled their orders, they would take a seat near the stove. In the fall, they'd pick up an apple before they sat down. In those days, they all carried a pocketknife. The apple got a good rub on the pants or sleeve, then it was time to peel.

The object of the peeling was to see how long you could make it without breaking. If you cut deep, the peeling could be too heavy. If you cut thin, it could be too fragile. It had to be just right.

The men would begin the slow, deliberate process by placing the point of the knife at the top of the apple, just inside the stem area. As they worked, the group gossiped about community news and swapped hunting and fishing tales. Once an apple was peeled, the long peeling was held up for everyone to see, and the others acknowledged the success with a nod. Then the peeling was tossed into the stove, and the apple sliced and eaten. Granddaddy often joined in. I can still see him standing in front of the stove with his white butcher's apron, an apple turning round and round in his hands.

Every time I peel an apple it brings back those heartwarming childhood memories. I have never been able to completely peel an apple without breaking the spiral of the skin. Maybe the blade on my paring knife is too dull or too wide.

Or maybe it's the fact that I'm not sitting behind that pot-bellied stove, taking the time to just sit and listen as I peel an apple.

Beverly Fox Freeman
Asheville, North Carolina

A young Beverly (above) adds to her fond memories of the grocery run by Granddaddy and Granny Young (top).

A Taste Of Summer

SINK YOUR TEETH INTO THE BEST BITES OF THE SEASON!

Summer Steak Kabobs

PREP: 20 MIN. + MARINATING • **GRILL:** 10 MIN. • **MAKES:** 6 SERVINGS

INGREDIENTS

½ cup canola oil
¼ cup soy sauce
3 tablespoons honey
2 tablespoons white vinegar
½ teaspoon ground ginger
½ teaspoon garlic powder
1½ pounds beef top sirloin steak, cut into 1-inch cubes

½ pound whole fresh mushrooms
2 medium onions, cut into wedges
1 medium sweet red pepper, cut into 1-inch pieces
1 medium green pepper, cut into 1-inch pieces
1 medium yellow summer squash, cut into ½-inch slices
Hot cooked rice

DIRECTIONS

1. In a large resealable plastic bag, combine the first six ingredients. Add beef; seal bag and turn to coat. Refrigerate 8 hours or overnight.

2. On 12 metal or soaked wooden skewers, alternately thread beef and vegetables. Discard remaining marinade.

3. Grill kabobs, covered, over medium heat 10-12 minutes or until the meat reaches desired doneness, turning occasionally. Serve with rice.

Grilled Veggie Sandwiches with Cilantro Pesto

PREP: 20 MIN.
GRILL: 20 MIN. + STANDING
MAKES: 4 SERVINGS

INGREDIENTS

- ⅔ cup packed fresh cilantro sprigs
- ¼ cup packed fresh parsley sprigs
- 2 tablespoons grated Parmesan cheese
- 2 garlic cloves, peeled
- 2 tablespoons water
- 1 tablespoon pine nuts
- 1 tablespoon olive oil

SANDWICHES

- 2 large sweet red peppers
- 4 slices eggplant (½ inch thick)
  Cooking spray
- ½ teaspoon salt
- ¼ teaspoon pepper
- ½ cup shredded part-skim mozzarella cheese
- 4 kaiser rolls, split

DIRECTIONS

1. For pesto, place cilantro, parsley, Parmesan cheese and garlic in a small food processor; pulse until chopped. Add water and pine nuts; process until blended. While processing, slowly add oil.

2. Grill peppers, covered, over medium heat 10-15 minutes or until skins are blistered and blackened, turning occasionally. Immediately place peppers in a large bowl; let stand, covered, 20 minutes. Peel off and discard charred skin. Cut peppers in half; remove stems and seeds.

3. Lightly spritz both sides of eggplant slices with cooking spray; sprinkle with salt and pepper. Grill, covered, over medium heat 3-5 minutes on each side or until tender. Top with peppers; sprinkle with mozzarella cheese. Grill, covered, 2-3 minutes or until cheese is melted; remove from grill.

4. Spread roll bottoms with pesto. Top with eggplant stacks and roll tops.

Italian Green Bean Salad

PREP: 20 MIN.
COOK: 15 MIN.
MAKES: 9 SERVINGS

INGREDIENTS

- 1½ pounds fresh green beans, trimmed
- ½ cup thinly sliced roasted sweet red peppers
- ½ cup fresh basil leaves, thinly sliced
- 3 tablespoons pine nuts, toasted
- 2 tablespoons plus 1¼ teaspoons olive oil
- 1 tablespoon lemon juice
- ¼ teaspoon garlic powder
- ¼ teaspoon pepper
- ⅛ teaspoon salt

DIRECTIONS

1. Fill a 6-qt. stockpot two-thirds full with water; bring to a boil. Add beans; cook, uncovered, 8-10 minutes or until crisp-tender. Remove beans and drop into ice water. Drain and pat dry.

2. In a large bowl, combine beans, peppers, basil and pine nuts. In a small bowl, whisk oil, lemon juice and seasonings until blended. Drizzle over bean mixture; toss to coat.

NOTE To toast nuts, cook in a skillet over low heat until lightly browned, stirring occasionally.

Mint Watermelon Salad

START TO FINISH: 20 MIN.
MAKES: 8 SERVINGS

INGREDIENTS

- 6 cups cubed seedless watermelon
- 2 tablespoons minced fresh mint
- 1 tablespoon lemon juice
- 1 tablespoon olive oil
- 2 teaspoons sugar

DIRECTIONS

Place watermelon and mint in a large bowl. In a small bowl, whisk lemon juice, oil and sugar until sugar is dissolved. Drizzle over the salad; toss gently to combine.

Grilled Corn with Dill

PREP: 15 MIN. + SOAKING
GRILL: 25 MIN.
MAKES: 10 SERVINGS

INGREDIENTS

- 10 medium ears sweet corn in husks
- 1 cup butter, softened
- 2 tablespoons minced fresh dill or 2 teaspoons dill weed
- 2 tablespoons minced fresh chives
- 1 teaspoon lemon juice
- 1 teaspoon Worcestershire sauce
- ½ teaspoon garlic salt
- ¼ teaspoon pepper

DIRECTIONS

1. Place corn in a stockpot; cover with cold water. Soak 20 minutes; drain. In a bowl, beat remaining ingredients until blended.

2. Peel back corn husks to within 1 in. of bottoms; remove the silk. Spread corn with butter. Rewrap corn in husks; secure with string.

3. Grill, covered, over medium heat 25-30 minutes or until tender, turning often. Cut string and peel back husks.

Fiery Tomatoes

PREP: 10 MIN.
COOK: 5 MIN. + CHILLING
MAKES: 8 SERVINGS

INGREDIENTS

- 5 large tomatoes, cut into wedges
- 1 medium onion, sliced
- ¾ cup white vinegar
- 6 tablespoons sugar
- ¼ cup water
- 3 teaspoons mustard seed
- ¼ teaspoon cayenne pepper
- 1 large cucumber, sliced

DIRECTIONS

1. Place tomatoes and onion in a large heatproof nonreactive bowl. In a saucepan, combine vinegar, sugar, water, mustard seed and cayenne; bring to a boil. Cook 1 minute, stirring to dissolve sugar; pour carefully over tomato mixture. Cool completely.

2. Stir in cucumber. Refrigerate, covered, overnight.

Summer Carbonara

PREP: 20 MIN. • **COOK:** 15 MIN. • **MAKES:** 6 SERVINGS

INGREDIENTS

- 1 package (16 ounces) spaghetti
- 2 tablespoons olive oil
- 1 large sweet onion, finely chopped
- 1 medium yellow summer squash, diced
- 1 medium zucchini, diced
- 2 garlic cloves, minced
- 4 plum tomatoes, seeded and chopped
- 2 large eggs, lightly beaten
- 1 cup grated Parmesan cheese
- 12 bacon strips, cooked and crumbled
- ¼ cup fresh basil leaves, thinly sliced
- 1 teaspoon minced fresh oregano
- ½ teaspoon salt
- ¼ teaspoon pepper

DIRECTIONS

1. Cook spaghetti according to package directions. Drain; transfer to a large bowl.

2. Meanwhile, in a large skillet, heat oil over medium-high heat. Add onion, squash, zucchini and garlic; cook and stir until tender. Add tomatoes; heat through. Remove from pan; keep warm.

3. Reduce heat to low. Add eggs to same skillet; cook slowly, stirring constantly, until eggs reach 160° and just begins to coat a metal spoon (eggs will be frothy; do not overcook). Add to hot spaghetti; toss to coat. Add vegetables and remaining ingredients; toss gently to combine.

Sweet Raspberry Tea

PREP: 10 MIN. • **COOK:** 15 MIN. + CHILLING
MAKES: 15 SERVINGS

INGREDIENTS

- 4 quarts water, divided
- 10 individual tea bags
- 1 package (12 ounces) frozen unsweetened raspberries, thawed and undrained
- 1 cup sugar
- 3 tablespoons lime juice

DIRECTIONS

1. In a saucepan, bring 2 quarts water to a boil; remove from heat. Add tea bags; steep, covered, 5-8 minutes according to taste. Discard tea bags.
2. Place raspberries, sugar and remaining water in a large saucepan; bring to a boil, stirring to dissolve sugar. Reduce heat; simmer, uncovered, 3 minutes. Press mixture through a fine-mesh strainer into a bowl; discard pulp and seeds.
3. In a large pitcher, combine tea, raspberry syrup and lime juice. Refrigerate, covered, until cold.

Grilled Potato Packets

PREP: 20 MIN. • **GRILL:** 45 MIN.
MAKES: 8 SERVINGS

INGREDIENTS

- 2 pounds medium red potatoes (about 7), cut into wedges
- ¼ cup thinly sliced green onions
- 6 slices ready-to-serve fully cooked bacon, chopped
- ¾ teaspoon salt
- ⅛ teaspoon pepper
- 2 tablespoons butter
- 1 cup shredded cheddar cheese

DIRECTIONS

1. In a large bowl, toss potatoes with green onions, bacon, salt and pepper. Place half of the mixture on a greased double thickness of heavy-duty foil (about 18 in. square); dot with 1 tablespoon butter. Fold foil over potato mixture and crimp edges to seal. Repeat to make a second packet.
2. Grill, covered, over medium heat 20-23 minutes on each side or until potatoes are tender. Remove from grill.
3. Open foil carefully to allow steam to escape. Sprinkle potatoes with cheese. Grill opened packets, covered, 3-5 minutes longer or until cheese is melted.

Yummy Zucchini Chocolate Cake

PREP: 20 MIN. • **BAKE:** 30 MIN. + COOLING
MAKES: 18 SERVINGS

INGREDIENTS

- 1¾ cups sugar
- ½ cup canola oil
- 2 large eggs
- ⅔ cup unsweetened applesauce
- 1 teaspoon vanilla extract
- 2½ cups all-purpose flour
- ½ cup baking cocoa
- 1 teaspoon baking soda
- ½ teaspoon salt
- ½ cup buttermilk
- 2 cups shredded zucchini
- 1 cup (6 ounces) miniature semisweet chocolate chips
- ½ cup chopped pecans, toasted

DIRECTIONS

1. Preheat oven to 350°. Coat a 13x9-in. baking pan with cooking spray.

2. In a large bowl, beat sugar and oil on medium speed 1 minute. Add eggs, applesauce and vanilla; beat 1 minute longer. In another bowl, whisk flour, cocoa, baking soda and salt; add to sugar mixture alternately with the buttermilk, beating just until blended. Stir in zucchini.

3. Transfer to prepared pan. Bake for 20 minutes. Sprinkle with chocolate chips and pecans. Bake for 10-15 minutes longer or until a toothpick inserted in center comes out clean. Cool in pan on a wire rack.

NOTE To toast nuts, bake in a shallow pan in a 350° oven for 5-10 minutes, or cook in a skillet over low heat until lightly browned, stirring occasionally.

S'Moreos

START TO FINISH: 15 MIN. • **MAKES:** 4 SERVINGS

INGREDIENTS

- 4 Oreo cookies
- 3 tablespoons creamy peanut butter
- 4 whole graham crackers, halved
- 1 milk chocolate candy bar (1.55 ounces), quartered
- 4 large marshmallows

DIRECTIONS

1. Spread both sides of each Oreo cookie with peanut butter; place over half of the halved graham crackers. Top with chocolate.

2. Using a long metal skewer or long-handled fork, toast marshmallows 6 in. from medium-hot heat until golden brown, turning occasionally. Place on chocolate; cover with remaining graham crackers. Serve immediately.

Red, White & Blue Cupcakes

PREP: 45 MIN. + CHILLING • **BAKE:** 15 MIN. + COOLING • **MAKES:** 4 DOZEN

INGREDIENTS

- 1 package yellow cake mix (regular size)
- 1¼ cups water
- 4 large eggs
- 1 can (14 ounces) sweetened condensed milk
- 1 cup coconut milk
- 1 can (5 ounces) evaporated milk
  Dash salt

WHIPPED CREAM

- 3 cups heavy whipping cream
- ⅓ cup confectioners' sugar
  Assorted fresh berries

DIRECTIONS

1. Preheat the oven to 350°. Line 48 muffin cups with paper liners.
2. In a large bowl, combine cake mix, water and eggs; beat on low speed 30 seconds. Beat on medium for 2 minutes.
3. Fill prepared cups halfway, allowing room in the liners for milk mixture. Bake 11-13 minutes or until a toothpick inserted in center comes out clean. Cool 5 minutes before removing from pans to wire racks.
4. Transfer cupcakes to baking sheets. Poke holes in cupcakes with a skewer. In a small bowl, mix milks and salt; spoon about 1 tablespoon mixture over each cupcake. Refrigerate, covered, overnight.
5. In a large bowl, beat cream until it begins to thicken. Add confectioners' sugar; beat until soft peaks form. Spread over cupcakes; top with berries. Refrigerate leftovers.

Hancrafted with Love

EASY IDEAS SHOW OFF SUMMERTIME JOY.

Tin Can Herb Set

Welcome summer with a tabletop herb garden made from upcycled soup cans.

WHAT YOU'LL NEED

- 3 recycled soup cans
- Metal pie plate
- 3 herb plants
- Potting soil
- Small decorative rocks
- Burlap ribbon, extra-wide
- Burlap lace ribbons, various widths
- Jute twine
- 3 flat wood ovals
- 3 wood skewers
- Card stock scraps
- 3 oval stickers, black
- Fine-point paint pen, white
- Drill
- Glue gun
- Craft glue

DIRECTIONS

1. Remove labels from cans. Wash cans with soap and water, removing any of the label residue.
2. Drill a small hole through the bottom of each can for drainage. Repot each plant in a can, adding potting soil as needed.
3. Wrap a piece of extra-wide ribbon around each can; overlap ends. Fold overlapping edge under to create a hem; hot-glue hem.
4. Wrap a piece of lace ribbon around the wide ribbon on each can, varying the lace widths among the cans, and glue as in Step 3, positioning the overlapped ends over the previous ends.
5. Trace wood oval on wide burlap ribbon and cut out 3 burlap ovals. Using craft glue, adhere a burlap oval to each wood oval, matching edges. Trim edges to neaten, if needed.
6. Hot-glue a border of twine around the burlap oval edges for a finished look.
7. For each plant marker, use paint pen to write the herb name on a sticker. Attach sticker to a card stock scrap, and trim card edge even with sticker. Hot-glue sticker assembly to the center of a burlap oval.
8. Hot-glue the blunt end of a skewer to the back of each assembled herb marker. Let dry completely.
9. Place plants in pie plate. Add markers. Arrange rocks around cans in pie plate as desired.

Twists of Charm

Kristy and Kelli of *LollyJane.com* gussy up plain old storage jars with colorful paints and pretty knobs. What a great way to present a hostess gift!

WHAT YOU'LL NEED

- Acrylic paint
- Foam brushes
- Multipurpose sealer
- Mason jars or old food jars
- Drill and bit
- Assortment of knobs with metal screw bases

DIRECTIONS

1. Paint jar lids, applying 2-3 light coats. When dry, apply sealer with a foam brush.
2. Drill through the middle of each jar lid with a drill bit. Screw knobs into place.

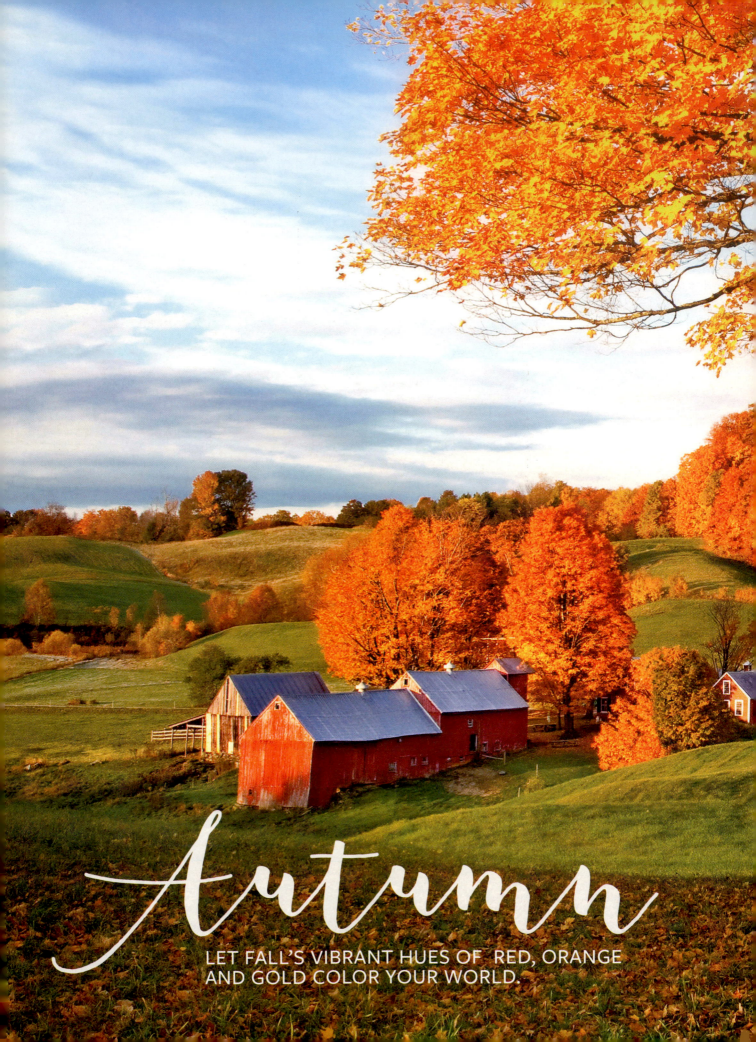

Autumn

LET FALL'S VIBRANT HUES OF RED, ORANGE
AND GOLD COLOR YOUR WORLD.

The Good Life

SIT BACK AND RELAX AMID FALL'S FINEST.

Smiling faces abound as hundreds of scarecrows take over this Washington farm.

DAN WILLIAMS

No Stuffed Shirts Allowed

Many farms sprout a few scarecrows in the autumn. However, Remlinger Farms, located in Carnation, Washington, boasts more than 500 of these greeters at its Fall Harvest Pumpkin Festival.

They beckon from the highway, welcome visitors to the farm and point out parking as well as the farm store, restaurant and restrooms. These scarecrows drive vintage tractors and wagons, hang by their knees from trees and operate antique trucks, plows, fire engines—even an old grindstone.

Billie and Jim Nelson create and deploy this happy-go-lucky fall workforce. Billie took over from the original scarecrow artist in the 1990s and enlisted the help of her husband. "Jim is the artist," says Billie, an employee at the farm for more than 30 years. "He paints on all of their faces."

Each year when the leaves begin to change and nights get cooler, Billie and Jim open the scarecrow dormitory above the machine shop to assess the health of the old hands. They revive stuffing and clothing and create new characters.

The couple attempt to make each scarecrow unique. Over the years, Jim developed several expressions, from grinning grown-ups to smiling toddlers, but you also will notice an occasional grimace, angry frown or wistful face. After all, the life of a scarecrow isn't all fun and games!

Once Jim finishes creating a face on the cloth head Billie has sewn, Billie begins securing buttons and zippers and sewing raffia to pant legs and sleeves. She stuffs the bodies with plastic bags, which hold up better than traditional straw in the wet Washington weather. Before the farm opens for the season, Billie and Jim transfer loads of scarecrows from the loft to the bed of their truck, then spend days setting up the stuffed workforce displays all over the 200-acre farm and surrounding rural roads. Visitors love to see scarecrows thumbing rides, sitting on fences and maneuvering old bicycles.

As with all scarecrows, garments are secondhand. But they're not just thrift store bargains. Billie uses many clothes that once belonged to the farm staff. Walk about the grounds with supervisors or park managers, and they'll point out a shirt and pair of pants worn by their toddler son or a cheerleader outfit that they wore in high school.

Bonnie Remlinger and daughter Diane, who handles the day-to-day operation of the farm along with Diane's husband, Will, are not spared the dubious distinction of having scarecrows model their old blouses and sweaters. Jeans, baseball caps and jackets can be traced to Gary Remlinger, Bonnie's husband and second-generation owner of the farm.

Billie herself joins the scarecrow legion during the fall festival. She puts on designer duds with fancy patches and Minnie Pearl-worthy straw hats. She and other guides point out the actual scarecrows lounging on fences and note: "My relatives—who just hang around while I work."

The Nelsons simply love watching farm visitors laugh at the scarecrows. When asked if she's ever been tired of scarecrowing, Billie says, "I'm here because I enjoy it."

It's fun to imagine that on some moonlit autumn nights, those 500 scarecrows hop down from their perches to hold a fall festival of their own. With all the character the Nelsons have given them, it wouldn't be a surprise.

Pam Williams
Bothell, Washington

"This cute pair of burrowing owls always showed up on my mail route. I finally stopped to take a photo of the two."
CHRISTIE JOHNSTON
WILDORADO, TEXAS

"I had to smile when I saw my good friends, little McKenzie and Steve the hired hand, heading out of the stable on a gorgeous day in Scottsdale, Arizona."
DON TROUT
CHARLOTTE, MICHIGAN

Autumn reminds us to enjoy the beauty, kindness and love that surrounds us.

Personal Pumpkins

Saturdays are always days for our family to visit Grandma and Grandpa Meyers' farm. There are tractors to sit on and fields to check, and around Father's Day weekend we plant pumpkins. The kids get a wagon ride, and then they help out by planting seeds or stepping on the ground after the seeds are well-covered.

All through the summer, we keep a close watch on the pumpkins' progress. When they're green and moderately sized, Grandpa pulls out his pocketknife and carves each grandkid's name in a pumpkin. He cuts only deep enough to pierce the hard rind. The large leaves that grow along the vine shouldn't be disturbed, so it can be quite challenging to see the pumpkin well enough to carve. The names grow bigger as the pumpkins grow.

The first time Grandpa did this was for Lacey, the oldest, when she was about 3 years old. He asked Lacey what was on that pumpkin, and her face lit up with a huge smile, although—oops!—Grandpa had forgotten the "e" in her name!

One year, one of the pumpkins never turned orange; another, a name was upside-down. Still, the kids love having their very own, unmistakable pumpkins.

Jessica Meyers
Union Grove, Wisconsin

"This Virginia scene reminds me of my first paying job at age 10. Paid per bale, I made enough to buy a baseball glove!"
JOMAR ALWES
LAS VEGAS, NEVADA

Even this pair of geese takes time to appreciate autumn's lovely weather.
PHOTO BY KATHY WRIGHT/ ALAMY STOCK PHOTO

"Our granddaughter Molly, 2, is always struggling to keep up with the older kids. Here, Claire, 5; Mason, 4; and Cruz, 3, climbed onto the fence hoping the horses would come near. Molly didn't quite make it up, but she certainly tried."
JOANNE WELLS
WEST LINN, OREGON

Amish Friendship Bread

Recently, I opened the door to a friend's frantic knocking. Tear-stained, with a Tupperware bowl clutched in her hands and her bottom lip trembling, she said, "Please, please take it."

I cautiously lifted the bowl out of her hands. "Oh, my! What is it?"

"Amish friendship bread. And you have to follow all of the rules."

Bread rules?

"Keep it comfortable; room temperature is best. Don't put the lid on too tight. Stir for the first five days. On Day Five, add one cup each of milk, flour and sugar. Stir for four more days."

I grabbed a pen and quickly started scribbling her many instructions.

"On Day Ten, feed it again. Keep one cup of the batter for yourself." She handed me a bread recipe. "Divide the rest among three containers for friends."

As she ran back to her car, she hollered, "But whatever you do, don't bring me any."

I lifted the lid and got a whiff of pure sewer gas. I snapped it shut and shoved it behind the toaster.

On Day Two, when I finally remembered to stir, I found that the starter had tripled in size, rupturing the Tupperware lid. Smelly globs had bubbled onto the countertop. I scraped what I could into the bowl and gave the batter an angry stir.

For days, I approached the beast with caution, hoping it wouldn't sense my apprehension. I fed it on Day Five and woke that night with a start, sensing something was wrong.

I tiptoed to the kitchen. My stinky companion had erupted yet again and was making its way across the counter, headed for the front door. I spent the rest of my evening scooping and wiping. By morning, I had it corralled in an ice cream bucket.

For the next 96 hours, I dared not leave the house for fear I'd return to find the creature oozing from the windows. On the hour, I stirred, carefully keeping the cat away lest he be swallowed whole.

By daybreak of Day Ten, I was dividing the mix into bowls and then speeding down the road in search of unsuspecting friends.

I raced home, elated to reclaim my kitchen, but as I pulled into the driveway I spotted a dish on my doorstep. A note read, "I offer you this starter batch of Amish friendship bread. Enjoy!"

It was signed, "Your friend." I didn't know who the culprit was, but I was pretty sure she wasn't Amish. And sure as sourdough, she was not my friend!

Ann Morrow
Custer, South Dakota

"Our son Lincoln shared a smile and a swing with his cousin, Caroline, on a warm fall Sunday."
JEDD MEDEFIND
MERCED, CALIFORNIA

Plump pumpkins tempt shoppers at Miller's produce stand in Bureau County, Illinois.
PHOTO BY TERRY DONNELLY

Farm-To-English Dictionary

After 30-plus years as a transplanted city girl, I have deciphered most "farmerisms" uttered by those working the land: folks like my husband, father-in-law and our neighbors. Here I'll explain some words and phrases encountered in conversation with farmers.

First, some things have multiple names. For example, chopper wagon, forage wagon and green-feed wagon are all the same thing. The difference between a hay elevator and a conveyor? Not much.

A dairy animal may have calved or freshened, but either way has just given birth. And manure is the same as...you get the idea.

And then there's a whole list of terms that are often misused by non-farmers. An udder is the whole bag hanging under the cow, not each little dangly, which is called a teat. Also, a heifer that has a "hot quarter" didn't just pull change out of the clothes dryer. That cow has an inflammation in one section of her udder.

Bulls are boy cows, from which I strongly urge you to keep your distance. If you think bullheadedness is an unfortunate trait in humans, imagine an actual bull head backed up by at least a ton of bull body.

Hay is feed, a mixture of grasses that have been cut, left to dry and baled. Straw is bedding, the stems of either oats or wheat that are left over after the combine removes the grain. (And despite these definitions, cows sometimes nibble at straw and lie down on hay.)

Tractors are usually diesel-powered and capable of pulling large implements and wagons. A tractor is not used to mow the lawn. It is a workhorse of a machine that, in this part of the Midwest, is usually John Deere green or International Harvester red. A good-natured rivalry exists between the supporters of each.

Then there are commonly used phrases in farmland.

Well, I s'pose... This indicates the end of a meal, a conversation or a rest period. It means, "I suppose we ought to get back to work."

Could you give me a hand a minute? For this "60 seconds of assistance," turn off the stove, make sure the kids are safe, put on work boots and grab a jacket.

Can I have a bandage? Either the wound is still bleeding after being wiped on a pant leg, or there's no duct tape handy. Be prepared to call the paramedics.

While you're in town, can you pick up a bolt? Even if you know the correct length and diameter, the store clerk will ask if it's metric or standard, fine or reverse thread, hardened, lag or carriage. In other words, buy every possible type of bolt, have your farmer pick out the right one, and return the rest later. (Or, if possible, simply bring along the bolt that needs replacing.) These techniques also apply to buying hoses, belts, tires and gaskets.

Cows are out! This announcement, generally shouted around midnight during a thunderstorm or a blizzard, means it's time to get up from a dead sleep and herd cattle that know full well you will never outrun them.

I hope these definitions are helpful. With some practice, the next time you find yourself in the midst of a farming conversation at an auction, county fair or feed mill, you'll be able to nod knowingly.

Well, we've been talking awhile, so I s'pose...

Linda Perona
Brighton, Wisconsin

The sights, sounds and aromas of fall beckon us to immerse ourselves in the season.

COUNTER CLOCKWISE FROM THE TOP:

"I took this picture on a day trip on the Mohawk Trail in Massachusetts. The old wooden barn against the colorful trees looked like a postcard."
Jennifer Kriegel
FRAMINGHAM, MASSACHUSETTS

"My son Jesse wanted to be a dairy farmer since he could walk. The look on his face here tells me he knows where he belongs—on the farm, with his animals."
Megan Galbraith
VALLEY FALLS, NEW YORK

"A friend and I took a drive to see the fall foliage when we spotted this line of simply beautiful orange trees."
Zelda Rowley
LANCASTER, PENNSYLVANIA

"After moving to an acreage closer to our family farm, my kids were delighted to find the hard work of pumpkin planting paying off. Zara was so happy to pick the first pumpkin from our patch."
Tyler Burton
WILLIAMS, IOWA

Autumn
Scrapbook

SEE WHY FALL STRIKES A CHORD IN THE HEART OF THE COUNTRY.

Venture outdoors for the chilly air, sweet fragrances and color displays of this popular season.

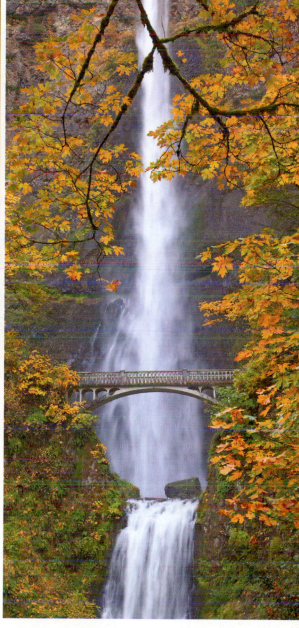

"I was at a farm photographing thistle plants when I stumbled upon more than a dozen American goldfinches."
BILL NIVEN
CHESAPEAKE, VIRGINIA

Bigleaf maples transform Multnomah Falls and the Benson Bridge into autumnal perfection in the Willamette Valley, Oregon.
PHOTO BY TERRY DONNELLY

PAUL REZENDES

Kayakers take advantage of a gorgeous morning in early fall to explore Bowman Lake, Montana.
PHOTO BY CHUCK HANEY

"My daughter, Paige, visited a farm to choose her own pumpkin, but she found more enjoyment in her first encounter with dandelions."
DEANNA BUNCH
SPOKANE, WASHINGTON

A cheerful collage of oak, beech, teaberry, maple and other leaves brightens up the autumn forest floor in New Salem, Massachusetts.
PHOTO BY PAUL REZENDES

This bridge in Alabama's DeSoto State Park affords a fine view of Indian Falls.
PHOTO BY PAT & CHUCK BLACKLEY

Crisp winds, earthy hues and childlike excitement signal the time to explore autumn's splendor.

"With the sun setting in the distance, a photo of my friend Jim and his daughter fishing was the best trophy I could ask for on a recent trip."
JERRY SIEMINSKI
AMBERG, WISCONSIN

"On Halloween, my grandson Levi wanted to wear his costume most of the day."
JANET KAPPERS
SPRING VALLEY, MINNESOTA

"Here's my dad teaching my son, Ben, how bees make honey by showing him the frames full of combs."
SARAH MCCARTY
MOORESVILLE, INDIANA

"After some squirrels began snacking on this pumpkin, I moved it from my front porch to the backyard. Next thing I knew, it had a hole right through it, and it became the fast food restaurant for the neighborhood."
JOE FABIAN
ST. CLAIR SHORES, MICHIGAN

Sunflowers reflect the very last bit of summer as cool fall winds begin to take over.
PHOTO BY MONICA BRILL
MOUNT MORRIS, NEW YORK

"I took this photo of a tufted titmouse from inside a garden shed that I converted into a bird blind."
LUCIAN PARSHALL
BRIGHTON, MICHIGAN

"My a-maze-ing sons, Henry and Steven, navigate a corn maze."
LORI EISERLE
NIANGUA, MISSOURI

This cheery-looking farm was built long before the Revolutionary War. The foothills of the Blue Ridge Mountains are the backdrop to a spectacular scene.
NANCY HOUCK
WATERFORD, VIRGINIA

"At first light, just after daybreak in Pendleton County, West Virginia, fall foliage in the George Washington and Jefferson National Forests takes on a spectacular golden glow."
AARON SHAVER
STAUNTON, VIRGINIA

In fall, nature takes hold of our senses, and we are grateful for the experience.

Weston's Antique Apple Orchard in Wisconsin is a living museum for heirloom varieties such as Ashmead's Kernel and Cox's Orange Pippin.
PHOTO BY DIRK VANOVER

"In late October, my wife and I were blown away by the beauty of the Genesee River Gorge in Letchworth State Park."
RONALD DRAPER
BUFFALO, NEW YORK

"The bobbing fun of these mallard ducks caught my eye one fall afternoon."
LAURA MEIER
BLOOMINGTON, MINNESOTA

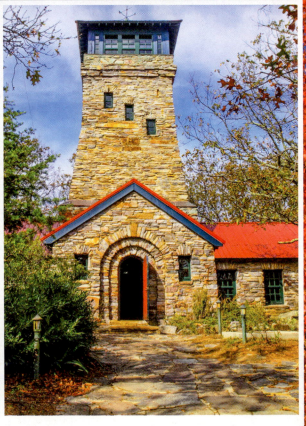

What a site—and sight! Here's a shot of the Alabama's Scenic Byways Bunker Fire Lookout Tower in Cheaha State Park.
PHOTO BY PAT & CHUCK BLACKLEY

Mount Moran in Grand Teton National Park looks even more majestic in fall.
PHOTO BY TERRY DONNELLY

Be thankful for the lovely days of autumn.
Their beauty fades far too quickly.

TERRY DONNELLY

Founded in 1814 as a utopian community, New Harmony, Indiana, is a walker's paradise in fall.
PHOTO BY MARSHA WILLIAMSON MOHR

"Every autumn I look forward to the migration of sandhill cranes through southeastern Tennessee. The weary travelers rest for a couple of months at the Hiwassee Wildlife Refuge near Birchwood."
DAN SOMMERS
CHATTANOOGA, TENNESSEE

Indiana is rich with historic structures, including the Hillsdale Covered Bridge in Tippecanoe County.
PHOTO BY
MARSHA WILLIAMSON MOHR

"My grandson, Colin, picked his pumpkin and enjoyed rolling it down a hill at a small farm in Pennsylvania."
JUDY AYDELOTTE
QUARRYVILLE,
PENNSYLVANIA

"I delight in traveling to the Great Smoky Mountains. This male white-tailed deer was walking in a field, looking for females. I guess I got his attention!"

SUE JARRETT
BEAUFORT, SOUTH CAROLINA

Autumn puts on a spectacular color show along the Virgin River in Zion National Park.
PHOTO BY DENNIS FRATES

Heart & Soul

GRATITUDE ABOUNDS THIS TIME OF YEAR.

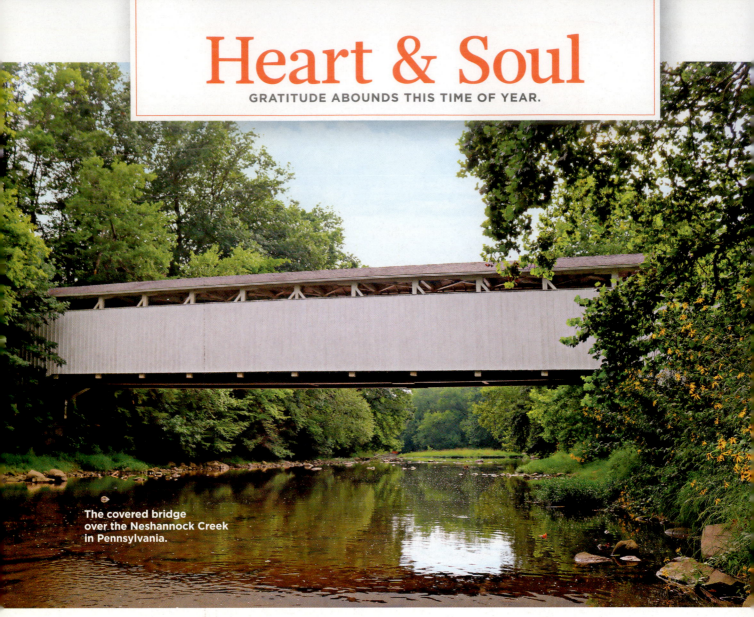

The covered bridge over the Neshannock Creek in Pennsylvania.

A walk through a covered bridge began one man's journey of a lifetime.

DAD AND BABY ON COUCH: NATHAN HOGUE

Walks of Life

Though not getting old by admission, I've hiked many country miles and caught enough fish to be considered a fisherman. Spanning so many of those steps and trout was a specific covered bridge that holds a spot in my heart.

This historic structure was not only a classroom for self-taught lessons in fly-fishing; my life's best moments have taken place on the bridge and the Neshannock Creek. From the time I was a boy dangling my feet into a cool farm pond, fishing seemed as natural and necessary as breathing. I have spent more time on the water than on land. Those who knew and loved me fully supported these passions, particularly my older brother, Nate.

On my 18th birthday, Nate gave me an Orvis fly rod—a gift he had bought with money earned serving our country. One October morning, Nate and I snuck in a fishing trip before his next deployment to the Middle East.

At first, both pieces of the fly rod trembled and the line flopped atop the water's surface. Embarrassed, I coached myself, "Marshall, whether you're using a bamboo cane pole, a spinning rod or a fly rod, they all serve the same purpose and the same master."

Suddenly, I found a rhythm and slowly added grace to each cast. Observing the line as it hit the water, I tried with all my wits to comprehend how the drift affected the fly and what the fish saw.

I did what any rookie would do. I threaded my line through whatever fly looked good. As drift after drift floated alongside us beneath the covered bridge, the line gave an unmistakable pause. Moments later a taut line led to a bent rod. Nate was in pure disbelief —I had tricked a trout within minutes.

I fooled more than a dozen on my first trip! Grinning from ear to ear, wading below the rod's slender silhouette on the white covered bridge, I smiled at my brother and said, "This is the best day of my life!"

Nearly a decade's worth of casts later, I'd live another best day. Like so many boys do, I became a man and met a girl. Laura was everything I dreamed. She was smart, honest, kind, funny and beautiful. When I wasn't pursuing trout on the creek, I was pursuing Laura.

One summer afternoon, Laura and I drove toward my old stomping grounds. I pulled off the worn road when we got to the bridge. Holding hands with Laura and admittedly scanning the water for trout, we walked and talked just long enough to lose track of the time.

We sat on the bridge's stone ledge. Just below us, years earlier I had first pulled a fly box from my vest. Now I fished in my pocket for a ring. Laura, reading my mind as easily as I read those waters, said in a loving voice, "I cannot imagine life getting any better than this!"

In the years since, I have become a father to the most perfect little girl, Leah. I decided the day she was born that she'd become my lifelong fishing buddy as soon as she could dangle her toes in a farm pond.

Around the time she turned 2, Leah and I were spending the day together, doing the things dads do with their daughters—laughing, getting ice cream and telling stories. I turned down the road I had known so well in my youth and took Leah for a walk to the covered bridge.

The April breeze helped part her strawberry blond hair as I knelt down to kiss her forehead and take her hand in mine. My child's hazel eyes, mirroring the green waters of the Neshannock, looked into mine, and she said, "Love you, Dadda!"

The unforgettable words echoed along the cut rocks and reverberated through the covered bridge as if it were a megaphone.

While it is true I only fish a mere fraction of what I used to, this seems to make me appreciate it much more. With my covered bridge, I, too, have come full circle. I held a rod with a brother, a ring with a woman and a hand with a daughter. All walks of my life were enriched by sharing them with those I love.

So find a bridge, take a walk and hold on, for your journey is just beginning.

Marshall Lynch
New Wilmington, Pennsylvania

Plans for Leah's (above) first fishing trip began when she was an infant in her father's arms (opposite, far left). Both Marshall and Laura share the outdoors with baby Leah (opposite right).

Patchwork of Our Lives

While visiting my husband's relatives, I admired his Aunt Doris' collection of hand-stitched quilts. A particularly beautiful one stood out from the rest.

Auntie explained that every piece of this quilt was cut from a favorite outfit and represented an important moment in her life. "The blue gingham is from a blouse I wore to the very first picture show I ever saw," she said. Then she giggled. "I let my beau hold my hand in the dark for the longest time.

"The yellow was a summer dress I wore to the carnival. The Ferris wheel seemed to go up forever. I was so scared! I closed my eyes, but my friend was strong and brave and held me till we got back down to earth."

Her stories went on. She was allowing me to see a very intimate part of her life. And when it was time to leave, she presented me with her cherished quilt.

On the ride home, I discovered, very carefully, that the quilt's filler is actually a blue woolen blanket from World War II marked "U.S. Army Issue." That's when my husband confided his own piece of Aunt Doris' story: She'd had a forbidden romance with a man who became a war hero.

I began retelling this touching story to my preteen grandchildren, but with some trepidation. Maybe children raised in the age of video games wouldn't be interested in an old lady's ramblings about an old blanket, but I wanted to pass along this valuable piece of family history.

My 12-year-old granddaughter loved the romance of it, after I explained why old clothes were used to make bed coverings. This opened the door to describing how mothers passed along their knowledge of cooking, gardening and sewing to ensure that their daughters were well-armed to face life's demands.

In turn, my granddaughter explained how modern mothers pass on knowledge of computers, college and financial planning to ensure their daughters' success as well. Then it was time for the boys. They were enthralled by the homecoming parties and parades for soldiers. My description of how the whole country came together in the war effort was met with great pride.

In turn, they explained that the internet now unites the whole world, so loved ones don't have to wait so long without word of a soldier's health. At this, I felt a catch in my throat.

Surprised by how much my grandchildren had to teach me, I thought of the days when multiple generations of families lived under one roof. Sharing knowledge and history must have been a daily occurrence. Maybe grandparents taught old-country culture to grandchildren, and grandchildren shared school lessons with their grandparents.

Multigenerational homes may be rarer now, but my grandsons' talk of the internet connecting the world showed me that technology could bring together not only soldiers and their families, but also could unite different generations.

We can use new ways to foster the love that grandparents and grandchildren have always shared. As long as we continue to teach and learn from each other, we can build closeness despite any time and distance that may separate us.

It can be anything—computers, cooking, gardening, art, maybe even a young lady's story told in an old bed covering—that brings you closer to all of those you love.

Rose Padrick
Cocoa, Florida

The Legend of Skunk Hollow

Halloween night found us kids scurrying along the dark, heavily wooded roads. A full moon peeked around tall oaks and maples, sometimes illuminating the path before us, other times casting across it eerie shadows that both scared and thrilled us.

Trick-or-treating was difficult around our rural Pennsylvania farm because of long walks between houses. Kindly local farmers knew this. Instead of a quick exchange at the door, they invited us in to warm up around the woodstoves. They treated us with big helpings of homemade goodies and fussed over our Halloween costumes.

The longest haul was along the road that went from my house to the Kulp farm, but it was my favorite. In those days, though the road had no official name, we knew it as Hollow Road. Dad called it "Skunk Hollow" to tease his good friend Mr. Kulp, who lived at the very end of it.

To us kids, it was the legendary Sleepy Hollow. We named it after the short story by Washington Irving that featured the fictional yet terrifying headless horseman character.

Five of us, ranging in age from 7 to 10 years old, were trick-or-treating together one particular Halloween. We scared ourselves silly by telling stories about the headless horseman, who surely lived in the neighboring woods.

As we neared the Kulp farm, we heard crashing and snorting among the trees. The sound of galloping hooves was headed straight for us. Frozen in fear, we were too scared to run. A creepy coldness ran up the back of my neck. Henry, age 7, finally broke the trance, running and screaming for all he was worth toward the Kulp farm.

Seconds later, two deer leapt out right in front of us. After we caught our breath, we laughed about how little kids like Henry could be so scared of deer.

By the time we got to the house, Mrs. Kulp had calmed Henry. She herded us into her big farm kitchen and plied us with her apple-butter glazed donuts and fresh hot cider from their King and Winesap apples. As we were leaving, she stuffed bags full of treats into our arms. Mr. Kulp saw we were tired and insisted on taking us home. He broke a bale of hay into the bed of his pickup and covered us with horse blankets. We arrived home filled with the warmth of good food and the knowledge that, as long as we had caring neighbors, we were safe from headless horsemen.

Pat Arbeiter
Grand Junction, Colorado

Our Front Porch

I can see so many things clearly from my front porch. Like the big old Black Angus bull way down there under that cottonwood tree. He's been busy swatting flies with his tail and playing tag with the blistering sun all day. The light cuts sideways and holds on hard while that burning fireball sinks into the Pacific Ocean. The bull will rest easy soon—a rush of cool air always comes down the canyon at dusk.

I can see the big cedar with the tree house that my grandson and I built years ago. I can still see us up high, pounding nails and laughing about Grammy telling him every half-hour or so not to fall.

From this old porch the rusty metal roof of the barn looks to have been part of the landscape forever. For a hundred years or more, in the heat of summer and cold of winter, it has provided shelter for every manner of creature. All found rest within the big, musty sanctuary. Beams of sunlight stream like lasers through the knotholes, and the sound of laughing children chasing each other over bales of hay echoes forever in my memory.

I can see into the past from this old porch. I see the look of delight on my grandfather's face when I'd come to visit him, seldom as it was. His words were kind and his love absolute. I smell mesquite in the air; I hear the wind in the hoodoos and the trickling sound of the Red River's Prairie Dog Fork as it passes in front of the old ranch house where I was born.

Grandparents, parents and siblings have all gone on, but their images linger on this porch. I can hear voices of the past floating in the soft breeze of twilight.

Reaching out, I take the hand of my darling. We sit and hold on to one another in the quiet shadows. Our hands are weathered and wrinkled, yet hers are forever tender. The image of a beautiful young girl stands facing me as I place a ring on her finger. Fifty years of her unwavering assurance provide the energy that sustains me.

The future is shrouded from view as always, and the number of sunsets we'll see remains unknown. Though one evening the cool air will come down the canyon, the heat and sorrows will give way, and we'll forever rest easy.

Kerry Taylor
Livermore, California

A Girl and Her Pony

For as long as I can remember, I have loved horses, and growing up I dreamed of owning my very own. In my mind's eye, I saw myself sitting high in the saddle on a beautiful, well-bred palomino and riding in a parade.

I was so sure I would get a horse for my high school graduation gift. The whole school year, I talked about it. I often asked my mother, "What kind of horse are you getting me?" She'd just smile and shake her head. Oh, well...I'll try another day.

On a warm morning in May of 1963, I looked out my bedroom window and saw a big Lane furniture truck pull up to our farmhouse, and I knew I had to forget about a horse and settle for a hope chest. Thank goodness for my wise mother; I was leaving home soon to start college—what would I have done with a horse? Still, the desire to own a horse never left me.

On another warm day many years later, my dream finally came true in the most unexpected way. Through the kindness of a scruffy-looking gentleman, I was blessed with an old stocky buckskin horse named...Buck. Yes, he was ugly and often temperamental, but he was a horse! Best of all, he warmed up to me, and I loved him.

One of the most memorable times I shared with old Buck was the day I got to ride him—with my husband, Ronald, by my side—in the Horse and Wagon parade hosted in our small town.

Early that morning, I brushed Buck until I thought my arms were going fall off, trying to make him look somewhat presentable, but it was hopeless. Still, nothing was going to stop me from riding him in that town parade.

Sporting my new cowgirl hat, gaucho pants and burgundy boots, I sat proudly in the saddle. I waited for the parade to start, my heart racing. I could hardly contain my excitement.

Finally the moment came! Wagon wheels began to roll, and horseshoes began to clop on the pavement.

And then it started to rain—not just a drizzle, but a heavy downpour. Ronald grinned at me from his own horse and asked, "Do you want to call it quits?"

"No way," I replied, rain dripping from the brim of my brand-new hat, "I've waited a long time for this day!" With that, we took to the parade route.

By the time the parade ended, my prized cowgirl outfit was drenched, and my boots were filled with water. How funny I must have looked! Our kids got a good laugh at our pathetic rain-soaked condition.

Poor Buck looked more pitiful than ever—a far cry from a beautiful palomino. But I was thrilled; he looked like a real champ to me. I was so happy, and Buck and my husband were right at my side. My dream of riding in a parade had come true at last.

Joyce Noel Wyatt
Kodak, Tennessee

Joyce and Buck wait for her dream parade to start. Little did she know Mother Nature had a surprise in mind.

The Pink Pumpkin Grower

Several years ago, Carol Holsopple-Froese was walking through her field when she spotted a sole pink pumpkin among a new variety of orange ones. What a lovely surprise!

To anyone who has battled breast cancer, such an encounter would be meaningful. But this 15-year breast cancer survivor is also a plant breeder and a co-owner of Colorado Seeds Inc. Carol and her husband have developed many plant hybrids, starting in the 1990s with a variety of seedless watermelon. The happy pink accident, however, is the closest one to Carol's heart.

After isolating the unique pumpkin's color characteristic into a full-fledged pumpkin cultivar, Porcelain Doll F1, Carol started the Pink Pumpkin Patch Foundation. Commercial growers donate 25 cents to breast cancer research for every pink pumpkin they sell.

Initially geared toward people producing pumpkins for grocery stores, the program for funding research really connected with farmers market growers, and it quickly took off.

Carol says her best success is working with the National Future Farmers of America Organization. The FFA partnership began with one group in 2013, and in a few years grew to between 80 and 90 chapters. "These young people are so articulate, involved and motivated because they have a teacher with breast cancer, or a mom or an aunt," Carol says. "It's uplifting to meet students who look beyond what affects them to help others."

A fairly small organization, Pink Pumpkin Patch focuses on a single mission—helping the researchers who lack funding. "These aren't the big-name people you always read about, but maybe they are the ones who are going to come up with a new therapy or make a significant step toward a cure," Carol says.

"We might think that $5,000, $10,000 or $15,000 isn't much, but maybe that's just what they need. Sometimes a little can go a long way," she adds.

To find pink pumpkins growers near you, donate or buy seeds, visit *www.pinkpumpkinpatch.org*.

Lorie West
Milwaukee, Wisconsin

Kansas FFA member Maggie Roth rallied fellow members to sell special pink pumpkins. Soon chapters in most other states joined the fundraising.

An unusual pumpkin in the patch led Carol Holsopple-Froese (left) to develop this pink variety, now used to fund breast cancer research.

Welcome to the Pink Pumpkin Patch, where scattered seeds help find a cure.

Fords Forever!

Grandpa's newly restored 861 recalls happy days on the family dairy farm.

I grew up on a farm that adjoins my grandfather's, which has been in the family since before the Civil War. My dad, Charles Smith, and grandpa, Craig Smith, each milked about 20 cows, and they worked together farming the 100 tillable acres on our 466-acre hilly, stony farm. They always had Fords.

In 1958 they traded in two Ford 8Ns, nicknamed Roy and Dale, for brand-new tractors. Grandpa got a Ford 861 Powermaster, and Dad got a 661 Workmaster. I was 9 years old the day we gathered to watch the dealer unload them off the truck.

I grew up with those two tractors—they were the only tractors on the farm from 1958 to 1970, when we bought a 1968 Ford 4000. But even after we started adding larger tractors, the 861 was the only one that could pull a chopper wagon up our steep hill in high gear. The 172-cubic-inch Red Tiger engine had plenty of torque, and the 861 didn't lug down like some of our newer tractors.

After Grandpa retired, I farmed with my parents for five years before moving on to a new career. But my four siblings and I still own most of the farm. My wife and I built our home on one corner, and we raised our four kids here. My years growing up on the farm were so nearly perfect that I can't help feeling nostalgic for the tractors.

The 661's motor blew up in the 1990s, and Dad sold it for parts—which he later regretted. But when my folks died, the 861 came to me. I spent 10 years happily restoring Grandpa's tractor, overhauling the motor and installing a new clutch, brakes and fenders. During the years between getting it running and getting it painted, I used it without a hood and fenders to plow snow, haul firewood and take the kids on hayrides.

I jokingly tell people that my wife knows not to come between my tractor and me, but I'm not sure she knows I'm joking. With so many good memories of the 861 and the time when it was so important to our lives and our livelihood, it's great to see it finally restored to its former red-and-gray glory.

Terry Smith
Rexville, New York

Terry's cousin and brother sit atop the new tractors in 1958 (top). Years later, Terry drives the refurbished Ford 861 during hay season.

A Taste Of Autumn

Thanksgiving Stuffed Turkey

PREP: 50 MIN. • **BAKE:** 4 HOURS + STANDING • **MAKES:** 24 SERVINGS (3 CUPS GRAVY, 16 CUPS STUFFING)

INGREDIENTS

- 1 turkey (16 to 18 pounds) with giblets and neck
- ¾ cup butter, divided
- ½ teaspoon garlic salt
- ½ teaspoon paprika
- 2 large onions, chopped
- 3 celery ribs, chopped
- 2 medium carrots, finely chopped
- 2 loaves (1 pound each) day-old egg bread, cubed
- 1 cup chopped fresh parsley
- 1 cup chicken broth
- ¼ cup egg substitute

GRAVY

- 1 medium carrot, halved
- 1 celery rib, halved
- 1 small onion, quartered
- 1 bay leaf
- 6 whole peppercorns
- ¼ teaspoon salt
- 4½ cups water, divided
- 6 tablespoons all-purpose flour

DIRECTIONS

1. Preheat oven to 325°. Reserve turkey giblets and neck; cover and refrigerate. Tuck wings under turkey; tie drumsticks together. Place turkey on a rack in a shallow roasting pan, breast side up. Melt ¼ cup butter; brush over the turkey. Sprinkle with the seasonings.

2. Roast, uncovered, until a thermometer inserted in thickest part of thigh reads 170°-175°, 4 to 4½ hours, basting every 30 minutes after the first hour. (Cover loosely with foil if turkey browns too quickly.)

3. In a large skillet, heat remaining butter over medium heat; saute the vegetables until tender. In a large bowl, combine bread cubes, parsley and onion mixture; stir in broth and egg substitute. Divide the mixture between two greased 2-qt. baking dishes. Bake, covered, until a thermometer reads 165°, about 30 minutes. Uncover; bake 10 minutes.

4. For gravy, place the vegetables, seasonings, 4 cups water and reserved giblets and neck in a large saucepan; bring to a boil. Reduce heat; simmer, covered, until giblets are tender, about 1 hour. Strain stock; return to pan.

5. Remove turkey from oven; tent with foil. Let stand 20 minutes before carving. Skim fat from pan drippings; add remaining drippings and loosened browned bits from roasting pan to stock.

6. Mix flour and remaining water until smooth; stir into stock mixture. Bring to a boil; cook and stir until thickened, about 2 minutes. Serve gravy with the turkey and stuffing.

Garlic & Herb Mashed Potatoes

PREP: 40 MIN. • **COOK:** 2 HOURS • **MAKES:** 10 SERVINGS

INGREDIENTS

- 4 pounds Yukon Gold potatoes (about 15 medium), peeled and cubed
- 1 package (8 ounces) cream cheese, cubed and softened
- ½ cup butter, cubed
- 1 cup (8 ounces) sour cream
- ⅓ cup heavy whipping cream
- 3 tablespoons minced fresh chives
- 1 tablespoon minced fresh parsley
- 3 garlic cloves, minced
- 1 teaspoon minced fresh thyme
- ½ teaspoon salt
- ¼ teaspoon pepper

DIRECTIONS

1. Place potatoes and water to cover in a 6-qt. stockpot; bring to a boil. Reduce heat; cook, uncovered, until tender, 10-15 minutes. Drain potatoes; return to the pot. Mash potatoes, gradually adding cream cheese and butter. Stir in remaining ingredients.
2. Transfer to a greased 3- or 4-qt. slow cooker. Cook, covered, to allow flavors to blend, 2-3 hours.

Easy Green Beans with Mushrooms

PREP: 10 MIN. • **COOK:** 5 HOURS
MAKES: 10 SERVINGS

INGREDIENTS

- 2 pounds fresh green beans, trimmed
- 1 pound sliced fresh mushrooms
- 1 large onion, finely chopped
- 2 tablespoons butter, melted
- 2 tablespoons olive oil
- 3 garlic cloves, minced
- ½ teaspoon salt
- ¼ teaspoon pepper
- ½ cup sliced almonds, toasted

DIRECTIONS

In a 6-qt. slow cooker, combine all ingredients except almonds. Cook, covered, on low until the beans are tender, 5-6 hours. Remove with a slotted spoon. Top with almonds.

NOTE To toast nuts, bake in a shallow pan in a 350° oven for 5-10 minutes, or cook in a skillet over low heat until lightly browned, stirring occasionally.

Sweet Potato Stuffing

PREP: 15 MIN. • **COOK:** 4 HOURS
MAKES: 10 SERVINGS

INGREDIENTS

- ¼ cup butter, cubed
- ½ cup chopped celery
- ½ cup chopped onion
- ½ cup chicken broth
- ½ teaspoon salt
- ½ teaspoon poultry seasoning
- ½ teaspoon rubbed sage
- ½ teaspoon pepper
- 6 cups dry bread cubes
- 1 large sweet potato, cooked, peeled and cubed
- ¼ cup chopped pecans

DIRECTIONS

1. In a 6-qt. stockpot, heat butter over medium-high heat; saute celery and onion until tender. Stir in broth and seasonings. Stir in remaining ingredients.
2. Transfer to a greased 3-qt. slow cooker. Cook, covered, on low until heated through, about 4 hours.

Roasted Balsamic Brussels Sprouts with Pancetta

PREP: 15 MIN. • **BAKE:** 30 MIN. • **MAKES:** 6 SERVINGS

INGREDIENTS

  2 pounds fresh Brussels sprouts, trimmed and halved
  3 tablespoons olive oil, divided
  ½ teaspoon salt
  ¼ teaspoon pepper
  2 ounces sliced pancetta or bacon strips, chopped
  2 garlic cloves, minced
  1 tablespoon balsamic vinegar
  ⅓ cup dried cranberries
  ½ cup pine nuts, toasted

DIRECTIONS

1. Preheat oven to 400°. Place Brussels sprouts in a 15x10x1-in. baking pan; toss with 2 tablespoons oil, salt and pepper. Roast 30-35 minutes or until lightly charred and tender, stirring halfway.

2. Meanwhile, in a large skillet, heat remaining oil over medium-high heat. Add pancetta; cook and stir 4-6 minutes or until crisp. Add garlic; cook 1 minute longer. Remove from heat; stir in vinegar.

3. In a large bowl, combine the Brussels sprouts, cranberries and pancetta mixture; toss to combine. Sprinkle with pine nuts.

NOTE To toast nuts, bake in a shallow pan in a 350° oven for 5-10 minutes, or cook in a skillet over low heat until lightly browned, stirring occasionally.

Drop Biscuits and Gravy

START TO FINISH: 20 MIN. • **MAKES:** 4 SERVINGS

INGREDIENTS

  1 cup all-purpose flour
  1½ teaspoons baking powder
  ⅛ teaspoon salt
  ½ cup 2% milk
  2 tablespoons butter, melted

GRAVY

  ½ pound bulk pork sausage
  1 tablespoon butter
  3 tablespoons all-purpose flour
  1¾ cups 2% milk
  ⅛ teaspoon salt
  ½ teaspoon pepper

DIRECTIONS

1. Preheat oven to 450°. Whisk together flour, baking powder and salt. In another bowl, whisk together milk and butter; stir into dry ingredients just until blended. Drop four biscuits onto a parchment-paper lined baking sheet; bake until golden brown, 10-12 minutes.

2. In a small saucepan, cook and crumble sausage over medium heat until no longer pink, 4-5 minutes. Stir in the butter until melted; sprinkle with flour. Gradually stir in milk, salt and pepper. Bring to a boil, stirring constantly; cook and stir 2 minutes. Serve over biscuits.

Turkey Salad with Pear Dressing

START TO FINISH: 25 MIN.
MAKES: 4 SERVINGS

INGREDIENTS
- 3 tablespoons olive oil
- 2 tablespoons lemon juice
- 1 tablespoon honey
- ¼ teaspoon salt
- ¼ teaspoon ground ginger
- 2 medium ripe pears, divided

SALAD
- 8 cups fresh arugula or baby spinach
- 2 cups cubed cooked turkey
- ½ cup pomegranate seeds
- ¼ cup chopped pecans, toasted
- ¼ cup dried cranberries
- 2 green onions, sliced
  Coarsely ground pepper

DIRECTIONS
1. For dressing, place the first five ingredients in a blender. Peel, halve and core one pear; add to blender. Cover and process until smooth.
2. Peel, core and thinly slice remaining pear. Divide arugula among four plates; top with turkey, sliced pear, pomegranate seeds, pecans, cranberries and green onions. Drizzle with dressing; sprinkle with pepper. Serve immediately.

NOTE To toast nuts, bake in a shallow pan in a 350° oven for 5-10 minutes, or cook in a skillet over low heat until lightly browned, stirring occasionally.

Maple–Almond Butternut Squash

PREP: 20 MIN. • **COOK:** 5¼ HOURS
MAKES: 10 SERVINGS

INGREDIENTS
- ½ cup butter, melted
- ½ cup maple syrup
- 4 garlic cloves, minced
- 1 teaspoon salt
- ½ teaspoon pepper
- 1 medium butternut squash (about 4 pounds), peeled and cut into 2-inch pieces
- ½ cup heavy whipping cream
- ¼ cup sliced almonds
- ¼ cup shredded Parmesan cheese

DIRECTIONS
1. In a 4-qt. slow cooker, mix first five ingredients; stir in the squash. Cook, covered, until squash is tender, 5-6 hours.
2. Stir in cream; cook, covered, on low until heated through, 15-30 minutes. Top mixture with almonds and cheese.

Apple Butter & Pumpkin Pie

PREP: 45 MIN. + CHILLING • **BAKE:** 45 MIN + COOLING • **MAKES:** 8 SERVINGS

INGREDIENTS

- 1¾ cups all-purpose flour
- ½ teaspoon salt
- ½ cup cold butter, cubed
- ¼ cup shortening
- 3 to 5 tablespoons ice water

FILLING

- 3 large eggs, lightly beaten
- 1 cup apple butter
- 1 cup canned pumpkin
- ⅔ cup packed light brown sugar
- ½ teaspoon salt
- ¾ teaspoon ground cinnamon
- ½ teaspoon ground ginger
- ¼ teaspoon ground nutmeg
- ¾ cup half-and-half cream

OPTIONAL TOPPINGS

- Sugared Cranberries (see note)
- Toasted chopped pecans
- Sweetened whipped cream

DIRECTIONS

1. In a bowl, mix flour and salt; cut in butter and shortening until crumbly. Gradually add ice water, tossing with a fork until dough holds together when pressed. Reserve one-fourth of the dough for cutouts; shape into a disk. Shape the remaining dough into a separate disk. Wrap each disk in plastic; refrigerate 1 hour or overnight.

2. On a lightly floured surface, roll large disk of dough to a ⅛-in.-thick circle; transfer to a 9-in. pie plate. Trim pastry to ½ in. beyond rim of plate; flute edge. Roll small disk to ¼-in. thickness; cut into desired shapes with floured 1-in. cookie cutters. Place the cutouts on an ungreased baking sheet. Refrigerate crust and cutouts while preparing filling.

3. Preheat oven to 425°. Mix eggs, apple butter, pumpkin, brown sugar, salt and spices; stir in cream. Pour into crust. Bake the pie on a lower oven rack 15 minutes. Reduce oven setting to 350°; bake until center is almost set, 30-35 minutes. Bake pastry cutouts on an upper oven rack until golden brown, 12-15 minutes.

4. Cool pie on a wire rack; serve or refrigerate within 2 hours. Decorate the pie with cutouts and toppings as desired.

NOTE To make Sugared Cranberries, place ⅓ cup sugar in a small bowl. In a microwave, warm 1 tablespoon light corn syrup, about 10 seconds; toss with 1 cup fresh cranberries. Add to sugar and toss; let stand on waxed paper until set, about 1 hour.

Cherry Chocolate Pecan Pie

PREP: 25 MIN. • **BAKE:** 40 MIN. + COOLING
MAKES: 8 SERVINGS

INGREDIENTS

- ¾ cup dried cherries or dried cranberries
- ½ cup brandy or cherry juice blend

CRUST

- 1¼ cups all-purpose flour
- 1 tablespoon sugar
- ¼ teaspoon salt
- ¼ cup canola oil
- 3 tablespoons 2% milk

FILLING

- ⅓ cup butter, softened
- 1½ cups sugar
- ⅛ teaspoon salt
- 3 large eggs
- ¾ cup all-purpose flour
- 1 cup chopped pecans
- 2 ounces semisweet chocolate, chopped
  Sweetened whipped cream, optional

DIRECTIONS

1. Preheat oven to 325°. Toss cherries with brandy; let stand, covered, 1 hour.

2. For crust, mix flour, sugar and salt. Whisk together oil and milk; add to flour mixture, tossing with a fork just until blended. Press mixture onto the bottom and up sides of a greased 9-in. pie plate.

3. For filling, drain the cherries, reserving 1 tablespoon brandy. Beat butter, sugar and salt until blended; gradually beat in eggs and reserved brandy. Stir in flour. Fold in the pecans, chocolate and cherries; pour into crust.

4. Bake until top is golden brown, 40-45 minutes. Cool on a wire rack. If desired, serve with whipped cream. Refrigerate leftovers.

Gran's Apple Cake

PREP: 20 MIN. • **BAKE:** 35 MIN. + COOLING • **MAKES:** 18 SERVINGS

INGREDIENTS

- 1⅔ cups sugar
- 2 large eggs
- ½ cup unsweetened applesauce
- 2 tablespoons canola oil
- 2 teaspoons vanilla extract
- 2 cups all-purpose flour
- 2 teaspoons baking soda
- 2 teaspoons ground cinnamon
- ¾ teaspoon salt
- 6 cups chopped peeled tart apples
- ½ cup chopped pecans

FROSTING

- 4 ounces reduced-fat cream cheese
- 2 tablespoons butter, softened
- 1 teaspoon vanilla extract
- 1 cup confectioners' sugar

DIRECTIONS

1. Preheat oven to 350°. Coat a 13x9-in. baking pan with cooking spray.

2. In a large bowl, beat sugar, eggs, applesauce, oil and vanilla until well blended. In another bowl, whisk flour, baking soda, cinnamon and salt; gradually beat into the sugar mixture. Fold in apples and pecans.

3. Transfer to prepared pan. Bake 35-40 minutes or until top is golden brown and a toothpick inserted in center comes out clean. Cool completely in pan on a wire rack.

4. In a small bowl, beat cream cheese, butter and vanilla until smooth. Gradually beat in the confectioners' sugar (mixture will be soft). Spread over the cake. Refrigerate leftovers.

Handcrafted with Love

BRING THE OUTDOORS IN WITH EASY AUTUMN DECOR.

Leaf Wreath

Use woodsy finds to create a wall accent with a pretty fall flourish.

WHAT YOU'LL NEED

Grapevine wire (double the length needed for desired wreath circumference)
Wire cutter
Leaves and other nature finds
Paraffin wax (see note)
Disposable pan
Waxed paper
Hot glue

DIRECTIONS

1. Collect fallen leaves, berry sprays, branches, acorns and pinecones. If needed, gently dry leaves, then lay on paper towels, covering with additional paper towels. Place heavy books on top to press leaves overnight.

2. Cut wax into small cubes with a serrated knife. Melt over low heat in a sturdy disposable pan. When wax is completely melted, remove pan to a heat-safe surface.

3. Dip each leaf into wax, swiftly coating front and back. Hold by the stem, keeping fingers away from hot wax. Place leaves on waxed paper to set.

4. Use grapevine wire to create wreath form, twisting the second length of wire around the first. Create a small loop of spare grapevine wire to hang wreath, and attach to top by twisting wire in place.

5. Arrange leaves and other finds, securing to wreath using hot glue.

NOTE: Heat wax slowly on a low setting—it will splatter if it gets too hot. Protect counters with towels and waxed paper. If a cloudy residue forms on top of melted wax, reheat until clear.

Sticks and Cones

Do-it-yourself scented pinecones make a dramatic centerpiece for your autumn table.

WHAT YOU'LL NEED

Pinecones
Birch or other branches
Wide-mouthed glass jar
Ribbon
Unscented witch hazel
Distilled water
Cinnamon essential oil
Clove essential oil
Plastic spray bottle
Plastic funnel (not for food)

DIRECTIONS

1. Insert funnel into top of open spray bottle. Pour in 2 tablespoons unscented witch hazel and 6 tablespoons distilled water. Add 10 drops cinnamon essential oil and 5 drops clove essential oil. Place spray cap on bottle. Shake gently until well mixed.

2. Gather pinecones and cut branches from outdoors or purchase these items. Lay pinecones on a flat, cleanable surface. Mist pinecones all over with scented spray and let dry. Place scented pinecones in jar, filling to brim.

3. Arrange the cut ends of branches among the pinecones. Wrap a length of ribbon around center of jar, knot in place and trim ends.

Cute Hoot

This happy little guy can't wait to join your family. Pam Kessler of *www.HouseofHawthornes.com* assembled him from recycled bottle caps, jar lids and utensils.

WHAT YOU'LL NEED

Large wood slice
Sawtooth picture frame hanger
E6000 glue
Branch
2 forks
Serving spoon
2 5-in. wide jar lids (see note)
2 regular canning jar lids with bands
2 bottle caps
Stain or Danish oil (optional)

DIRECTIONS

1. The wood slice can be left untreated, or if desired use stain or Danish oil to darken it. Let dry. Before assembling the owl, attach a picture hanger on the back of the wood.

2. Glue branch across the bottom of the wood slice, then glue the forks with tines overlapping the branch, as if the owl is perched there. Glue the spoon toward the top of the wood slice to resemble a beak.

3. Glue wide lids to the wood. Take the regular canning lids out of their metal bands and flip discs over to show the prettier side. Glue on top of the wide lids, then attach pop bottle caps as pupils.

NOTE: If you prefer a smaller owl, scale the lids to the size of the wood slice.

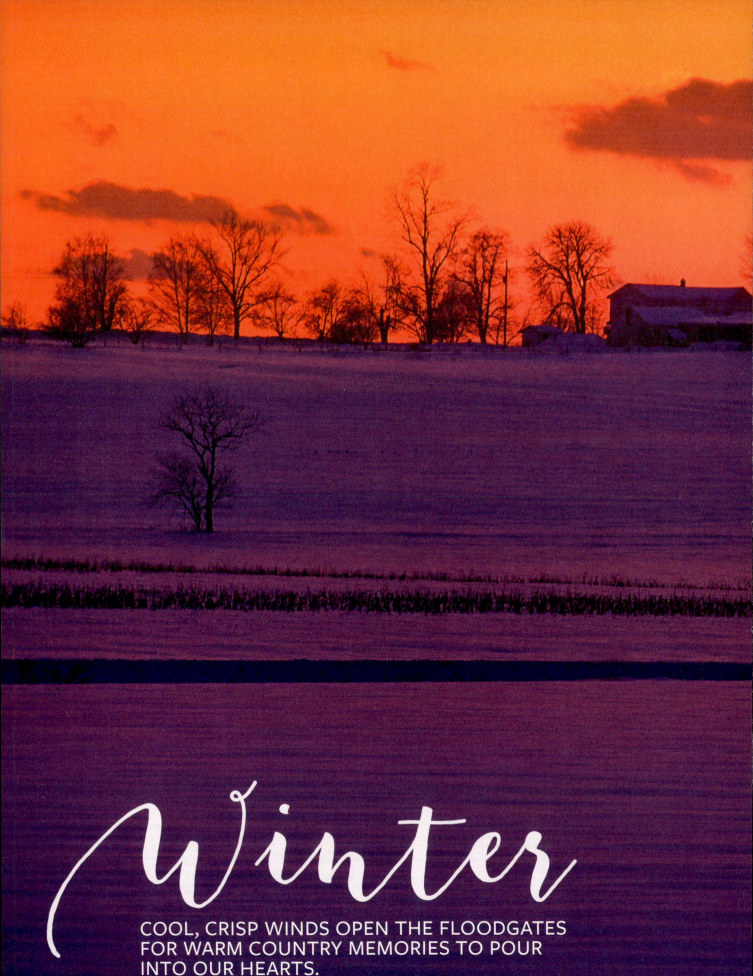

Winter

COOL, CRISP WINDS OPEN THE FLOODGATES
FOR WARM COUNTRY MEMORIES TO POUR
INTO OUR HEARTS.

The Good Life

CELEBRATE THE GLORY WINTER HAS TO OFFER.

Thirteen trees grew into a family business filled with cherished memories and traditions.

A Christmas Spirit That Grows and Grows

My family Christmas memories include my parents making wreaths and garlands, and my siblings and me helping customers find the perfect trees.

Werner Tree Farm sits on the edge of Middlebury, Vermont, and has about 20,000 trees of a dozen or so species spread over 36 acres. The farm got its start when my grandfather, Fred Werner, gave my parents 13 tiny Scotch pines left over from a planting project of his own. Since then, the business has branched out to include mail-order fresh wreaths and custom greenery. Our family operation has grown into one of the most popular cut-your-own tree farms in the state.

Farming is hard work, but we love growing trees as a family. Each spring and early summer, we plant saplings to replace those that were cut in the winter. In summer and fall, we trim and shape each tree with our shearing knives. In November, we convert my father's wood shop into a Christmas store. From the week before Thanksgiving until Christmas Day, our lives revolve around gorgeous evergreens.

We begin the selling season by heading to the mountains to gather brush for wreaths and garlands and to harvest trees for our precut racks. The whole family, along with a hired crew of elves, spends a few long days harvesting—often through cold, rain or snow. We bring more than 500 balsam and Fraser fir trees down from the mountains, plus a couple tons of balsam boughs.

Then my mother and I start making and decorating wreaths. With one or two hired helpers, we handcraft more than 500 wreaths in a year. That's a lot of early days and late nights drinking hot cocoa and listening to Christmas music on the radio!

Because we're so busy, we don't have Christmas customs such as ice skating parties, caroling or watching The Nutcracker. But we do have a unique Christmas tree-cutting tradition.

It started back when my sister Jessie and I were maybe 10 and our brother William was 13. It had been a busy year, and my parents hadn't gotten around to putting up our Christmas tree. Jessie, William and I decided we'd waited long enough, and it wasn't going to happen in time for Christmas if we left it up to our parents. All three of us regularly helped customers cut down and carry trees back from the field, so we decided we could do the same for ourselves.

We waited for our parents to go to bed before tiptoeing down the stairs. After putting on our coats and boots, we walked down the driveway with a bow saw and flashlight. My sister had seen a balsam-Fraser hybrid earlier that day while helping a customer, and she assured us it was the only one that would do.

It was a mild December night with plenty of moonlight. We took turns cutting, and then my brother and I picked up the trunk while my sister carried the tip. The walk home felt much longer, and the exhilaration of being out after dark faded as the tree got heavier. The house stayed dark as we got the tree standing almost straight before going to bed, quite pleased with ourselves.

Since then, it's become a tradition for us kids to set up the tree after our parents go to bed. We're grown now and my siblings have moved away, so we've had to move our outing to Thanksgiving, to make sure we're all there for the nighttime excursion.

The variety of Christmas tree may change from year to year, but the walk home takes us back to our childhood spent among the trees.

Amanda Werner
Middlebury, Vermont

The Werner Tree Farm (opposite top) sits at the edge of Vermont's Green Mountains. Anna Tracht (opposite far left) creates one of the 500 Christmas evergreen wreaths, while staff members harvest some of the trees (opposite left). As children, Will, Amanda and Jessie Werner began working the farm with mom Cheryl (below) and later at the store (right).

Blessings of a Winter Morning

It's still dark when the alarm in my head goes off. I roll out of bed and turn off the actual alarm—I beat it again. Just because I'm awake doesn't mean that my husband and daughter have to be up yet. It's my turn to milk.

In a few minutes, I'm ready to go. I slip on my muck boots and zip up my army surplus work coat. I tap my pockets and find my pocketknife, my keys and an open spot for my cell phone.

The Gator can't make it through the snow, so I pull out the orange sled my nephews were fighting over yesterday, place the bucket of udder wash on one end and set the portable milking machine in the middle. The milker is heavy when it's empty and a nightmare when it's full.

The sky glows with a light shade of indigo behind a sprinkling of stubborn stars. There's no sound except for the crunch of snow under my feet and the shushing sound of the sled. Still, Dot hears me coming and ambles over to the gate to meet me. Her dark brown eyes meet mine, and I swear she winks at me as she stretches out her neck for a good chin scratch. "Good morning, hooligan," I say as I rub her cheeks. Dot's calf, Polka, shyly watches from the barn door.

Dolly gives me a loud moo from her stall. She wants her breakfast, and she is not a patient girl. Grain is poured, Dolly is tied, udders are washed and the

milker is hung on its belt. I flip on the power, and the loud SHH-SHH SHH of the vacuum hose and the metronome beat of the pulsator fill the barn. I lean against Dolly's side as we wait. She is warm and soft and still.

When the milking is done, I turn off the machine, and the barn sits silent for a moment, until Dolly bellows for her calf, Daphne. I unhook the milker from the belt and groan under the weight of it. While waddling out to the sled I estimate that Dolly gave us at least 2 gallons of milk.

The stars are gone now, but the moon still hangs in a clear sky turning pink to the east. For a moment, I just breathe and feel the ache in my arm from the weight of the milker and its bounty. Everything is waking up. The chickadees and blackbirds are out in force, singing their morning songs. I close the gate behind me and watch Daphne and Dolly meet in the middle of the pasture.

The sled crunches across the snow. As I approach the house, the dogs race out the door, and I can't help smiling as I kneel down to hug them both. It was my turn to milk, my turn to watch the night turn to morning, my turn to gaze at the moon while the winter sun rises.

Rebecca Lane
Tunkhannock, Pennsylvania

Our Christmas Star

When our son Jeff was in seventh or eighth grade, the sisters at his school asked if we could provide one of our lambs for their annual Christmas pageant nativity scene. They wanted to use a real baby and live animals.

We said yes, of course, but we warned them that most of our ewes lambed in February, so we didn't have baby lambs in December. (That's me in the black-and-white photo below with one of our sheep.) The closest thing we could offer was a partly grown sheep that had been born too late for us to sell at Easter. He was large and not at all tame. That didn't worry them, but it worried us. The sisters had no idea how sheep react when they're scared.

My husband, Fred, started working with the lamb in hopes of taming him a little before the play. He also got him all cleaned up for his public debut. When the day arrived, the lamb still wasn't very tame, but he was beautiful. He had wool the color of butter, a black nose and hooves that were as black as coal.

Fred was working that night, so Jeff and I went out to the barn to load our nativity lamb into the station wagon for his trip to nearby Newry, Pennsylvania, and St. Patrick School. It was a beautiful, cold, clear night. Fred had separated the lamb into its own pen so he'd be easier to load. But the lamb, which wasn't used to being handled, let alone riding in station wagons, broke loose and started running around the barn.

So of course all 60 ewes started running wildly from one side of the barn to the other. It wasn't a very promising start. But Jeff waited patiently for the sheep to calm down, and we finally got the lamb loaded up. The school had set up a place for the lamb to wait just offstage. We put a leash around his neck, and I went to sit with the rest of the audience, hoping for the best.

My heart was in my throat as they led the lamb onto the stage to stand next to a crib with somebody's baby inside. I was downright scared that a sudden move or flashbulb would startle him and he'd run wild.

But to my amazement, he stood sweet and still for the entire play, which lasted about an hour. Somehow, I felt that maybe he was proud to be involved in this representation of a great event. He wasn't born in time to be sold as an Easter lamb, but he ended up with an even greater part to play.

Shirley Diehl
Duncansville, Pennsylvania

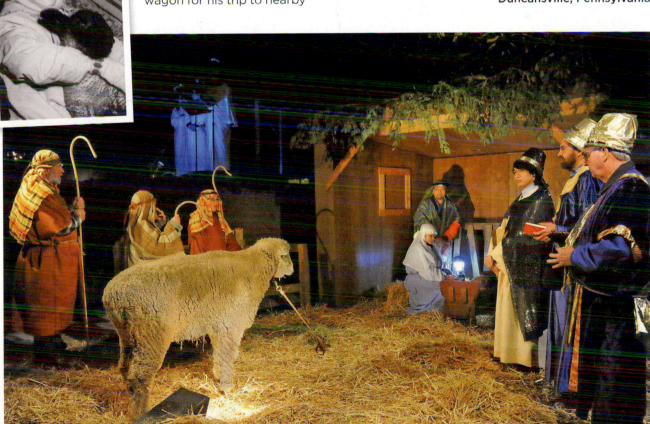

Giddyup, Let's Go!

When we purchased our first vis-à-vis carriage in 2005, my husband, Nick, and I didn't even have a place to store it or a horse to hitch up and pull it.

Shortly thereafter, we bought a house with a small barn to begin our adventure. And now we operate Dayze Gone Bye Carriage Rides, providing scenic tours of the surrounding Big Valley Amish country.

Since that first purchase, we have added several more carriages, an Amish buggy, a six-passenger spring wagon, a Conestoga wagon for larger groups and a pony wagon to use with our pony, Kidd. We also acquired two Percheron draft horses and two regular carriage horses.

Nick and I are both drawn to the nostalgia of earlier times, so in November 2009 we decided to search for an antique sleigh to add to our fleet.

The search took us south to Lancaster County, an area with several Amish buggy shops. What better place to look for a sleigh than an area where farmers still use horse-drawn equipment? Nickel Mine Coach Shop in the small community of Paradise happened to have an antique sleigh in the attic, but it was separated into many pieces.

The Amish owner, Christian Petersheim Jr., brought the sleigh down to show us. All the parts were there, and I could see that it must have been a beautifully painted sleigh at one time.

The sleigh's emblem read Sturtevant-Larrabee Co., Binghamton, New York, a renowned 19th-century carriage and sleigh manufacturer.

After much discussion on price and how much it would cost to bring this gem from the late 1800s back to life, we knew in our hearts that the investment would be well worth it.

Mr. Petersheim asked us what we wanted the sleigh to look like. We knew the seat should be vinyl so it wouldn't stay wet. We chose to have the body painted black, with gold pinstriping and snowflakes added. The runners and shaves would be burgundy. And we needed sleigh bells added, too. The complete restoration took two weeks.

Though we now had a barn and pasture for our horses, the 2-acre property was not large enough to host sleigh rides. We asked our neighbors, Eli and Esther Peachey, if we could use their fields, and they graciously granted permission.

But we had to figure out how we would move the sleigh from our barn to the Peacheys' farm down roads that get salted and plowed—great for cars, not so great for a sleigh.

With that in mind, we visited another Lancaster County shop, Shady Lane Wagons, where we located a frame with wheels attached.

Back to Nickel Mine we went. Mr. Petersheim determined that he could cut and weld this undercarriage to fit the antique sleigh's runners. So now we can drive our sleigh from our barn to the farm with the wheels attached if the roads have been plowed and salted. If they're covered with snow, Nick rides the horse pulling the sleigh. Our customers meet us at the Peachey's farm.

The day after we picked up the restored antique from Nickel Mine we were treated to a heavy snowfall. Our first ride in a one-horse open sleigh was an unforgettable experience!

Since that first winter, we have had the honor of fulfilling many bucket lists and hearts' desires. I love to stay behind and take photos. They look like magical scenes from Currier and Ives paintings set in a rural small town that time forgot.

Tara Richtscheit
Allensville, Pennsylvania

Tara and Nick could see the potential in the antique sleigh (below). At right, visitors create special memories on a wintry ride.

Nick, daughter Amanda and their horse Lynda trot through a winter wonderland.

A dash through the snow helps their guests revisit Christmases past in a one-horse open sleigh.

Guests of Nick and Tara enjoy a sleigh ride through scenic Amish country.

January Gift

The present was not packed in a box or delivered by mail. It wasn't wrapped in fancy paper or tied with a ribbon, but it was cloaked in vivid blue and rusty red feathers.

In the midst of a snowstorm on Jan. 20, 2014, an icy wind was howling, and the temperature hovered in the single digits. I looked out my sunporch window and couldn't believe my eyes. Four chubby bluebirds were sitting in the lilac bush. Their feathers were all plumped up as they tried to capture every bit of warmth they could find.

I was convinced the birds must have been blown off course, because I had never seen bluebirds at my home. What a blessing that they became frequent visitors to my feeders over the next few weeks!

Last year, conditions were quite different on Jan. 20. The temperature was a balmy 38 degrees beneath a cloudless blue sky. As I prepared for my afternoon walk, I glanced out the sunporch window. There, once again, sitting in the same lilac bush, were four truly brilliant bluebirds.

I looked closer and realized there were two pairs. The females' plumage is slightly subdued compared to the males', but they still stand out against the snow with their distinctive blue bodies and red breasts.

No other bird here in New England displays this combination of vibrant colors.

I consider bluebirds to be a precious gift from nature, in part because they visit so infrequently, but also because they remind me of summer days at my childhood home on Prudence Island. Back then bluebirds were plentiful in the island's open fields.

Bird lovers are making efforts to entice bluebirds to return to northern Rhode Island, where they have been rare for many years, and I'm very much rooting for their success.

However, I must accept that my feathered friends don't like to make their home in my woodsy environment. I don't have the open fields that bluebirds prefer for nesting, and there is no ideal spot to hang a bluebird house in my yard.

Even if they won't take up residence, I'm happy whenever they drop by for a winter snack. The four that have appeared at my feeders the last two Januarys were a delightful surprise. My heart soared, and I remember thinking it didn't matter if the sun was shining or the snow was swirling, because their cheery call was a reminder that spring would soon be here.

My positive thinking helped me get through winter's final push. The week after the birds appeared last year, we were in the midst of a blizzard that left behind over 2 feet of drifted snow. It was just the first of many snowstorms the bluebirds and I would endure before spring finally did come again.

I wonder what January will bring. Hopefully the bright, cheerful bluebirds will visit me once again.

Debbie Kaiman Tillinghast
Chepachet, Rhode Island

Let the crystal-clear beauty of winter leave you simply breathless.

COUNTER CLOCKWISE FROM THE TOP:

"I took a break from chores to take a photo of the sun rays streaming through a 100-year-old pear tree."
Maggie Bright
MONROE, WASHINGTON

"I was amazed by this pond, glistening in silver. To me, it was the epitome of a winter wonderland."
Zelda Rowley
LANCASTER, PENNSYLVANIA

"The birds at our feeders attracted this owl, but it spent most of its time on our swing set, watching us through the window."
Donna Pollard
WORCESTER, VERMONT

"I love visiting Jim and Kathy Ritcher's farm outside Cream, Wisconsin. They host an annual hayride at Christmas that starts at their beautiful barn."
Roberta Czaplewski
AUSTIN, MINNESOTA

Winter Scrapbook

GRAB A CUP OF COCOA AND ENJOY THE SEASON!

Let the glorious snow arrive! It flash-freezes nature's best and locks its beauty in our hearts and minds.

"On a trip to **Estes Park, Colorado**, we found this big fellow napping in the snow next to our cabin."
BUTCH BURKHARDT
RICHMOND, INDIANA

It's a great day for sledding in Wisconsin!
PHOTO BY R.J. HINKLE/ALAMY STOCK PHOTO

"Snow painted the nearby Marshville area a magical winter wonderland against a brilliant blue sky."
DANIEL COPE
SALEM,
WEST VIRGINIA

"Hoarfrost-covered branches highlighted splashes of color in our stark winter landscape."
KALLIE KANTOS-FRITZ
INTERNATIONAL FALLS, MINNESOTA

"This Belgian draft horse is all spruced up for Christmas."
CINDY ESHLEMAN
JONESTOWN, PENNSYLVANIA

An intense storm turned these huge spruce trees near Lake Superior into snowy ghosts.
PHOTO BY GARY ALAN NELSON

Explore a world like no other after the snow covers all with a brilliant touch of whimsy.

This classic Western barn houses horses and hay on El Rancho Pinoso near Pagosa Springs, Colorado.
PHOTO BY
CHRISTOPHER MARONA

"I spied this white-breasted nuthatch just hanging around on our peanut butter pinecone. It was a treat for the nuthatch, and a treat for me, too."
RUSS ERHARD
VAN BUREN, ARKANSAS

Take a breath of clean, crisp air and delight at the natural sensations this glorious season offers.

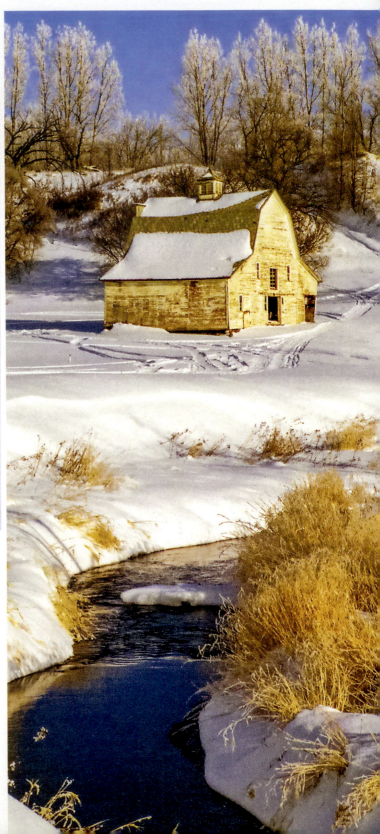

"This squirrel was playing in the snow on my patio. When I opened my sliding door, she rushed over to me and stood up with a begging look, as if to say, 'Can you come out and play?'"
CARI POVENZ
GRANDVILLE, MICHIGAN

"I was surprised to find this quiet brook running freely after Christmas."
DAVID PAUKERT
MICHIGAN, NORTH DAKOTA

"One day, the blue jays fought more than usual over the seed I place in the middle of my grapevine wreath. The blue jay on the left hunkered down, determined not to be bullied away."
SUSAN GEORGE
AVOCA, MICHIGAN

"This pasture in Winesburg, Ohio, shimmers in the sun after an ice storm."
EMILY RYERS
MUNGER, MICHIGAN

Midnight blue recedes as morning light awakens Longs Peak and Mount Meeker in Rocky Mountain National Park, Colorado.
PHOTO BY ERIK STENSLAND

"In the middle of an ice storm, I snapped this photo just as the tufted titmouse was looking at me."
MELISSA PERICH
POTTSTOWN, PENNSYLVANIA

"Charlie's favorite spot is at the window, where he can sit and survey the wintry yard."
MARY ANNA COLEY
OXFORD, NORTH CAROLINA

Winter explorers in snowshoes leave tracks through the pristine powder, daring us to follow them into the forest at Anthony Lakes, Oregon.
PHOTO BY DENNIS FRATES

You couldn't find a more downhome holiday scene than this snowy barn in West Granby, Connecticut.
PHOTO BY PAUL REZENDES

Let the goodness of Christmas warm your heart all year long.

A dad and his girls bring home the perfect tree to stand beside the fireplace in their Colorado home.
PHOTO BY DESIGN PICS INC/ ALAMY STOCK PHOTO

This adorable yellow Lab is going to make this Christmas the best ever for one lucky family.
PHOTO BY TERRY WILD STOCK

"It snowed overnight, and in the morning, I found this cardinal waiting for her turn at our feeder."
FAY SERBIAN
PORTAGE, PENNSYLVANIA

"It was a proud moment when my twins, Lindsey and Morgan, were old enough to hold their own candles during 'Silent Night' at our church on Christmas Eve."
KATIE CHALMERS
CLARENCE, NEW YORK

"I found an old sled at the top of the grain building on our 1800s farm. We fixed it up, and now when the kids are done sledding, they hang it in our small cow barn."
MARIE HILL
WOODSFIELD, OHIO

"We were decorating the house, so my son Michael wanted to wear his Santa costume. When he stopped to pet his horse, Zan, I captured the touching bond between them."
TRISHA GOETTLE
AVON, MONTANA

"Our horses, Hawk and Freckles, stay nice and warm under their blankets on a frosty December morning."
KATHY WEISSGERBER
TERREBONNE, OREGON

This leaf seems frozen in time at Allemansrätt Park in Minnesota.
PHOTO BY GARY ALAN NELSON

Dressed as a cowboy, a snowman gives farm visitors in Palmer, Alaska, a cheery hello.
PHOTO BY DESIGN PICS INC/ ALAMY STOCK PHOTO

You just can't beat the holly-jolly feeling of a downhome Christmas in the country!

Heart & Soul

EXPERIENCE THE TRUE MEANING OF A COUNTRY CHRISTMAS.

Listen carefully at midnight and you might just hear the barnyard animals talk.

Do You Hear What I Hear?

When I was 5 years old, everything was possible, especially at Christmas. That Christmas Eve, my three brothers and I sat around the tree while Mother brought us hot chocolate and cookies.

"There's a legend," she said, "that on Christmas Eve, a wonderful thing happens, but only if you believe." We scooted a bit closer.

"If you give all the animals extra feed and you're very quiet," she said, leaning in, "at midnight, for just one minute, all the animals in the world can talk."

"The animals can talk?" I whispered. How wonderful!

"If you can stay awake long enough, we'll all put on our coats and boots and go to the barn later," Mother promised.

Shortly before midnight, we bundled up and followed Mother into the night, the snow crunching under our boots. The sky was never so clear, the stars twinkling like a thousand diamonds, the moon a luminous pearl.

The animals seemed surprised to see us. We threw hay and oats into the mangers, then stood quietly, holding our breath. Mother pointed at her watch and nodded. It was midnight!

We strained to listen but heard only animals chewing and the occasional snort from a horse.

"I guess we didn't hear them," Mother finally said. "Maybe my watch was wrong and we missed it. But we can try again next year."

We all should have been disappointed, but we brimmed with excitement. Next Christmas, we might be the only people in the world who had ever heard animals talk!

The snow sparkled in the moonlight, the pines cast dark shadows, and the icy pond shone like an enormous silver mirror. The boys started throwing snowballs at each other, and Mother and I joined in. It was magical, being out after midnight and playing in the snow with Mother. She seemed so young as we ran after the boys, all of us laughing so hard that we could barely keep from falling down.

Every year after that, we repeated the ritual. Midnight on Christmas Eve we'd gather in the barn, smiling at one another, waiting for the animals to talk.

We grew older, and still we all walked to the barn late Christmas Eve. The smell of the hay, the warmth from the animals' bodies, the solid strength of the huge barn—every detail added to this singular moment we treasured in the harmony of farm and family.

The year before my brother left for college, I tried not to cry, knowing our family would probably never be wholly together on Christmas again. One by one we moved away, and while we often came home for the holidays, it was never again all of us at once.

After I married and we had four children, I began re-creating Mother's Christmas magic on our farm. It quickly became a tradition to take turns saying that the clock must be wrong, and we must have missed them by just a few minutes: we'd try again next year.

Somehow, the years flew by, and then it was my children growing up and moving away. Once again, I tried not to cry.

But then more years passed, and before I knew it my first grandchild, Colt, was 5, just as I was that first magical night. My son Pete and his wife, Rebecca, brought Colt and 3-year-old Shiloh, my second grandchild, for their first holiday on the farm that year.

It was early evening when I fixed hot chocolate as we all sat around the Christmas tree. I smiled and said quietly to Colt and Shiloh, "There's a legend that something wonderful happens every Christmas Eve, but to see it, you have to believe…"

**April Knight
Federal Way, Washington**

WINTER: HEART & SOUL   **173**

Guitars for Everyone!

Christmas Eve 2007 was an unforgettable day for our family. It was the day my dad, Leon Royal of Evening Shade, Arkansas, gave each of us one of his handmade acoustic guitars—14 in all for his three children, their spouses and eight grandchildren.

The living room was filled with guitars and grateful hearts. Some of us were strumming. Some of us were just taking in the incredible beauty of the instruments he'd crafted from different woods in various patterns and styles.

I am his youngest daughter, and I speak for the whole family when I say that Dad's guitars are a special gift that money cannot buy.

Seriously. Money cannot buy them. Despite many offers, he has sold very few over the years, preferring to build them for the pure enjoyment of working with wood, his hands and music.

Dad started playing the guitar when he was about 12 years old. His mother and father showed him a few chords, and he took it from there, playing along to the old music radio shows.

His grandpa Daniel Barnett had a fiddle that he'd made for himself many years before, which inspired Dad to build his first guitar in 1972.

He won't even guess at how many guitars he has made since then.

When Dad was raising a family, he only had time to build about one a year. The work goes faster now than when he had three children underfoot in his workshop, he says. Since retiring from the U.S. Postal Service, he's averaged six to eight a year.

Guitars aren't his only handcrafted masterpieces. He has also built mountain dulcimers, hammered dulcimers and dobros. He's even tried his hand at building electric guitars. While he enjoys building the electronics that go into the electric kind, he prefers the pure sound of his flat-top guitars.

Dad is a perfectionist. He wants his guitars to be beautiful and well-made, with a sound that's "just right." A true craftsman, he made the molds, forms, work boards and jigs that he uses to build his guitars. He hand carves the notched bracing inside the body and uses small chisels to work in the inlays that embellish the outside.

One day I asked Dad why he decided to give so many guitars away to us instead of selling them. In his modest and quiet way, he replied, "I just want my family to have a keepsake."

Angela Sutherland
Concord, Arkansas

Angela's dad made a dobro for his son James (right), and he shares the joy of music with the entire family at Christmas (below).

The Magic of Simple Gifts

Mom was diagnosed with stage 4 lung cancer in November of 2012, and I feared the next Christmas would be her last. I wondered what kind of a gift I could possibly give her to show her how much I loved her. Then it dawned on me—I could give her a card shower. I put a note in my Christmas cards asking friends to send Mom and Dad a card to lift their spirits.

Well, my little idea spread exponentially, thanks to my daughter and social media. She posted the request for cards on her Facebook page. In turn, her friends picked up the idea and shared it with their friends.

Near the end of November I asked Mom if she had been getting any Christmas cards. She said she had gotten a few, and I could tell by her voice she was wondering why I had asked. Well, the deluge began in early December. Some days the mail carrier delivered a bag of cards to their front door because he could not fit them into Mom and Dad's rural mailbox.

We live about a hundred miles from my parents and visited every week after she was diagnosed with cancer. Mom saved the cards she received each week so I could look at them, too. It became our weekly ritual.

We would sit at the kitchen table, and she'd read every card, often marveling at how pretty it was. Sometimes Mom had to rest, because there were too many cards for her to take in at once.

Then small gifts began arriving in the mail—books, candy, fruit and Christmas ornaments. Crafters sent beautiful homemade cards, some so fancy they were works of art. Teachers sent cards from their students, wonderfully cute crayon drawings with sweet sentiments. Mom especially loved those. They always made her smile.

Christmas cards arrived from almost every state in the union, along with cards from Germany, France, Australia, England, China, Switzerland, Japan, Italy and Canada. It was as though the world had come to visit her little farm. We talked about where the cards came from. Mom was continually amazed that these total strangers would take the time to send her a card along with their well wishes and heartfelt prayers.

The response was astounding, beyond anything I could have imagined. Mom received more than 1,200 Christmas cards. Whenever someone came by for a visit, she would proudly show them. It was the best Christmas present ever for my parents—and a welcome diversion from the reality of Mom's cancer.

Sadly, Mom passed away in early March 2013. I smile as I remember her opening her cards, and her total delight as she looked at every one. The cards were like little gifts to her. They remain a testament to the thoughtfulness of friends, relatives and many wonderful strangers. They're also a testament to the power of love.

Roxanne Rowley
Manistee, Michigan

The Frozen Schoolmarm

In May of 1951, I completed a one-year course that certified me to teach in a country school. That summer I was hired to teach—and live—in the Horseshoe Bend School, 9 miles northwest of Okaton, South Dakota.

My cot and camping stove were in one corner of the schoolhouse and my "indoor plumbing" was under the bed. The only running water came from a hand pump in the entry. The building had no electricity or telephone, but it did have a new oil heater to keep the chill off. The students and I sat huddled around it on the coldest days of the worst winter I've ever seen.

Snow was on the ground in December, but the weather didn't get really bad until the first big blizzard hit in January. It closed school for a week while the snowplows cleared the roads. Then school resumed until a February blizzard piled snow on top of snow. With drifts 10 and 12 feet deep, we lost another week of school while the roads were being cleared.

Classes resumed for two or three more weeks before the worst blizzard of all hit in March.

I've never seen snow accumulate as fast as it did that day. Parents came early to pick up their children.

The family that came the farthest got stuck in the snow before they made it home, I learned later. Luckily, it was in their driveway.

Meanwhile I was stuck at the school, completely alone. I had a battery-powered radio, but I couldn't listen very long without running down the battery.

So I did a lot of reading. With drifts up to 18 feet deep, even a bulldozer couldn't push the snow up the hill east of the school. They had to drive the Caterpillar across the fields to the top of the hill so they could push the snow downward. By the time they got the roads open, I was living on crackers and jelly.

When the snow finally began to melt, the roads turned to gumbo mud and once again became nearly impassible!

Even so, one morning I decided I needed a break, so I walked 5 miles to visit my sister and her husband on their farm. One of their neighbors kindly gave me ride back to the school on the hood of his Ford tractor.

That fall I decided to go back to college so I could teach at a school in town!

Darlene Woods
Chamois, Missouri

Even today,
Moma's doll
brings Linda joy.

Linda and
brother Roger
as children.

Christmas Dreams

My favorite Christmas happened when I was 4 years old. Back then it was just me, my little brother, Roger, and Moma, living just up the road from our grandparents and uncles. Roger and I knew that there wasn't much money, and Moma was rather upset that she couldn't give us a Christmas dinner, tree and presents.

So when I came across a Raggedy Ann doll in a magazine, I never said anything to Moma, but I did tell my grandma I thought this was the grandest doll ever. Grandma was surprised, because I never liked dolls. I was more attuned to tomboy things—toy gun holsters, cowgirl gear and anything to do with horses or farm equipment. But somehow Raggedy Ann touched my heart; she looked alone and like she needed someone, and I thought surely that someone was me.

Our grandpa cut down a beautiful tree for us, and we made decorations by stringing popcorn and gluing construction paper into a colorful garland. For the top, Moma cut out a cardboard star, which we covered with a piece of aluminum foil she had saved. She also drew pictures of Santa for us to color, and we put our Christmas lists on the back. Moma said that lots of children asked Santa for toys and that we shouldn't be greedy, but remember others.

I hope I never forget this Christmas Eve, how it felt to be warmed by the potbellied coal stove, potatoes baking on top of it, as snow gently piled up outside. Moma was busy making a huge apple stack cake, plus fresh fried pork, milk gravy and redeye gravy, and buttermilk biscuits to sop it up. Moma sang "Jingle Bells" while she worked, and all too soon it was bedtime.

I awoke Christmas morning to the smell of bacon and a warm hug from Moma. She smiled and told me to hurry up and get dressed because she thought she heard something on the roof. "I'm betting it's Santa," she said. "I think he's about to take off for home at the North Pole."

I ran to the kitchen window and looked out over a field dotted with hemlock trees, everything blanketed in snow, but no Santa. I turned around and softly, sadly, said that I guess we missed him. Moma turned me back to the window—there was Santa! And he was upside down! He was hanging over the roof to peek inside our house.

"Please don't fall!" I yelled. "Please don't leave! Let me get my brother." I ran to get Roger and crashed into him on my way, then I pulled him to the kitchen.

Santa was still there, and he asked for cookies for his long journey home. I was suddenly sad, because I didn't think we had any. As I opened my mouth to say so, Moma handed us each a bag, then opened the window so we could hand them out. Cookies in hand, Santa gave a big "Ho-ho-ho!" and disappeared from sight, sending a puff of snow cascading down from the roof. We turned to Moma, realizing he didn't leave any presents for us.

We thought maybe Santa had run out of gifts, but we decided Christmas was OK without presents. We were warm, we had plenty of food, we had each other. And we'd just given Santa Claus his cookies in person!

A loud knock on the door, followed by Moma swinging it open, revealed that Santa (played by my Uncle Tony) hadn't forgotten us. He brought a beautiful Raggedy Ann doll for me, and for my little brother a matching Raggedy Andy. On top of that, there was lots of fruit, along with peppermint and coconut stick candy.

Moma had lovingly sewed these dolls by hand, using all the material and yarn she had, in stolen moments and late nights. Her love made the dolls' green hair and multicolored bodies much prettier than the dolls I'd seen in the picture. Hand-sewn Raggedy Ann was my best friend, and I still have her, along with the best Christmas memories anyone could wish for.

Linda Bilbrey-Miller
Grimsley, Tennessee

A Tiny Piece of Tinsel

Growing up, we never had an artificial Christmas tree—or a cut one, for that matter. Instead, shortly before Christmas, my parents would haul in a balled or potted evergreen that we'd add to the landscape after the holidays. Daddy said it made "good cents." Mother said it was a meaningful tradition.

After we maneuvered the heavy tree into the house, Mother would conceal the bulky container with white flannel to make it look like snow. Daddy would string the lights, and over the tree's boughs, my sister and I would drape red and green paper chains, strings of popcorn and cranberries, and other baubles we fashioned out of shiny milk-bottle caps. Then we would hang tinsel until our tree sparkled.

It took a long time, but decorating the tree was an exciting family event, and after we finished we'd gather around the piano to drink eggnog and sing Christmas carols.

On a warm Saturday morning after New Year's Day, we'd all go into the backyard, pick a site and plant our Christmas tree, making sure to water it thoroughly to protect it against the January freezes that were sure to come our way.

Each year, the yard got a little woodsier as we continued to add new spruce or pine specimens. On summer afternoons when we'd play croquet or hide-and-seek in our evergreen grove, it was fun to discover birds' nests in the branches and recall "this Christmas" or "that Christmas." Best of all, on warm evenings, we loved to sit in lawn chairs and watch the fireflies flit in and out of the branches, as if trying to create their own Christmas tree light display.

One summer afternoon—some 40 years later—I drove by that childhood home and slowed down to savor the memories. The new owners were working in their yard, but when they saw me they stopped and came over to talk. When I told them that I had grown up there, they took me on a tour. The porch, front door and fireplace looked exactly the same. The kitchen had been updated, and the screened-in back porch was now a four-season room. When we walked into the backyard, I caught my breath and fought back a tear. I was standing in a forest. The couple explained they were from California and had been drawn to the home because of the huge evergreens out back.

When I walked over to admire a Colorado blue spruce, a glint of silver caught my eye. I could hardly believe it, but sure enough, a strand of weathered tinsel was still wrapped around a branch, sparkling in the brilliant sun.

Somehow, through almost half a century of Oklahoma heat and cold, that remnant of our holiday tradition survived, much like my fond memories of our backyard Christmas trees—memories that have become more treasured with each passing year.

Vivian Stewart
Piedmont, Oklahoma

"Don't Worry, Old Girl"

It was a cold, icy February afternoon on our cattle ranch in the flat, scabrock and sagebrush country of east-central Washington. My husband, Kris, had gone to visit a friend, and I was determined to show him that I could handle the ranch while he was away.

I had already fed the cows and busted the ice on our homemade 20x20-foot concrete water troughs once that day when I headed out with my 5-year-old daughter at about 2 p.m. to check them again. I tagged two new calves in the first herd, five in the second and four in the third. By that time, my daughter was sound asleep in the warm truck. So I slipped quietly out of the truck to break the ice in the water tank—and found a large black nose and two eyes sticking out of the trough.

One of our Angus cows had apparently tried to get to the running water hose on the far side of the 3-foot-deep tank and had fallen through the ice. I hopped up onto the ice, relieved to find she was still alive. "Don't worry, old girl. I'll get you out of there," I promised as I chopped at the ice in front of her.

When I had a bit of a path cleared, the cow tried to stand up. I heard a cracking sound, and suddenly I was almost waist deep in freezing cold water. Worse, the cow was too old, cold and weak to stand. I had to get her out of there soon or she'd die.

So I ran to the barn to get the tractor and loader, my freezing coveralls getting stiffer with each step. I managed to get a couple of chains around the cow and lift her out of the tank. She struggled to stand but couldn't make it. I had to get her dry—now!

I hastily searched the pickup for something to dry her off with. No luck. So I took off my jacket and started rubbing her, hard. After a few moments, she began to shiver, which I took as a good sign. Soon, the jacket was soaking wet and starting to freeze. I took off my sweatshirt and rubbed her with that.

She shivered more violently and tried to stand. When the sweatshirt was soaked, I took off my T-shirt.

By this time I'd been working on her for a good 20 minutes, and her body was about as dry as it was going to get. I started rubbing her legs; I could hear her teeth grinding in pain, but at least she was getting some feeling back. When my T-shirt was soaked, I took off my thermal wool undershirt and frantically rubbed some more. Darkness was setting in, and I had to get the cow up and moving quickly.

Then suddenly, she struggled to her feet. As the cow walked slowly, unsteadily back to the herd, I tossed my wet clothes into the truck bed and climbed into the cab. I realized I was shivering worse than the cow. As the door closed, my daughter woke up and asked in a sleepy voice, "Mom, where are we?"

"Checking the cows, sweetie."

She rubbed her eyes, gave me a strange look and asked, "Why are you wearing only a bra?"

Dawn Nelson
Creston, Washington

Rescue missions aren't new for the Nelsons. Here, Kris rescues a calf in a spring blizzard.

My Other Grandmother

We adopted Grandma's best friend as family.

Eleanor Joyce was not related to us, but she and my grandmother Esther Solseng were as close as sisters for 57 years. Eleanor was born in 1919 on her parents' farm in Thief River Falls, where she lived for 94 years. She loved everything about her homestead and even fell in love with and married her father's hired hand, George Joyce. The couple stayed there for decades, raising chickens, cattle and grain.

Eleanor and Esther became fast friends almost as soon as my grandparents moved nearby. They were nearly inseparable, but even more so after they both became widows. It was a rare occasion when they weren't together, especially in the kitchen. They loved to cook and bake side by side. One of my favorite memories is watching them make lefse. There was no recipe, just incredible culinary teamwork.

My grandmas were always there with advice and even hands-on help. When I wanted to impress my husband by making his family recipe for the Norwegian cookie called fattigman, Eleanor and my grandmother, both in their 80s, came to the rescue. We spent a fun-filled day rolling out and frying the cookies in lard—and sampling them, too!

My grandmother never drove, but Eleanor did, so when they weren't in the kitchen, they would hop into Eleanor's Rambler and drive all over the countryside looking for wildlife to watch or seeking a nice dress shop or a lunch café. After my grandmother turned 70, she and Eleanor took their first plane trip, to Arizona, and they both caught the travel bug. They visited Arizona several times, took an Alaskan cruise and even traveled to Germany.

In 2000, my grandmother passed away at age 90, and Eleanor was heartbroken. She had always worried about who would take care of her in her old age, since she had no children. She didn't need to worry. Lots of neighbors and close friends were there to help, especially my dad and mom. Everyone who was connected to Eleanor by heartstrings swooped in, taking her shopping and to doctor appointments, and helping her with home repairs and finances.

Eleanor lived life to its fullest right up to the end. She spent her very last weekend celebrating Mother's Day with my family, lavishing us with attention and an enormous feast, which she called "a little lunch." We always left her side with full hearts and warm hugs.

Michelle Benton
Thief River Falls, Minnesota

When Eleanor was a young farmer (top) she bonded with my family and stayed close to me and my sister (above) through the years.

Eleanor shared her kindness with all around her, including her dog, Pal, in the 1960s.

A Taste Of Winter

CELEBRATE THE SEASON WITH THE COMFORTS OF HOME.

Brie Puff Pastry

PREP: 15 MIN. • **BAKE:** 20 MIN. + STANDING
MAKES: 10 SERVINGS

INGREDIENTS

- 1 round (13.2 ounces) Brie cheese
- ½ cup crumbled blue cheese
- 1 sheet frozen puff pastry, thawed
- ¼ cup apricot jam
- ½ cup slivered almonds, toasted
- 1 large egg, lightly beaten
  Assorted crackers

DIRECTIONS

1. Preheat oven to 400°. Cut Brie round horizontally in half. Sprinkle bottom half with blue cheese; replace top.
2. On a lightly floured surface, roll pastry into a 14-in. square. Trim corners to make a circle. Spoon jam onto center of pastry; sprinkle with almonds. Top with Brie.
3. Lightly brush edges of pastry with beaten egg. Fold pastry over cheese, pinching edges to seal; trim excess pastry as desired.
4. Transfer to an ungreased baking sheet, seam side down. Brush pastry with beaten egg. Bake 20-25 minutes or until crust is golden brown.
5. Immediately remove from pan to a serving plate; let stand 45 minutes before serving. Serve with crackers.

NOTE To toast nuts, bake in a shallow pan in a 350° oven for 5-10 minutes, or cook in a skillet over low heat until lightly browned, stirring occasionally.

Herb Quick Bread

PREP: 15 MIN. • **BAKE:** 40 MIN. + COOLING
MAKES: 1 LOAF (16 SLICES)

INGREDIENTS

- 3 cups all-purpose flour
- 3 tablespoons sugar
- 1 tablespoon baking powder
- 3 teaspoons caraway seeds
- ½ teaspoon salt
- ½ teaspoon ground nutmeg
- ½ teaspoon dried thyme
- 1 large egg
- 1 cup fat-free milk
- ⅓ cup canola oil

DIRECTIONS

1. Preheat oven to 350°. In a large bowl, whisk together first seven ingredients. In another bowl, whisk together egg, milk and oil. Add to flour mixture; stir just until moistened.

2. Transfer to a 9x5-in. loaf pan coated with cooking spray. Bake until a toothpick inserted in center comes out clean, 40-50 minutes. Cool in pan 10 minutes before removing to a wire rack to cool.

Bacon–Wrapped Shrimp

PREP: 25 MIN. + MARINATING
BROIL: 5 MIN. • **MAKES:** 2½ DOZEN

INGREDIENTS

- 30 uncooked shrimp (31-40 per pound), peeled and deveined
- 6 tablespoons creamy Caesar salad dressing, divided
- 15 bacon strips, halved crosswise
- 2 jalapeno peppers, seeded and thinly sliced

DIRECTIONS

1. Preheat broiler. In a large bowl, toss shrimp with 4 tablespoons dressing; let stand 15 minutes.
2. Meanwhile, in a large skillet, cook bacon over medium heat until partially cooked but not crisp. Remove to paper towels to drain; keep warm.
3. Remove shrimp from marinade; discard marinade. Top each shrimp with a jalapeno slice and wrap with a bacon strip; secure with a toothpick. Place on a greased rack of a broiler pan.
4. Broil 4 in. from heat 2-3 minutes on each side or until shrimp turn pink, basting frequently with the remaining dressing after turning. Discard toothpicks before serving.

NOTE Wear disposable gloves when cutting hot peppers; the oils can burn skin. Avoid touching your face.

Stuffed Asiago–Basil Mushrooms

PREP: 25 MIN. • **BAKE:** 10 MIN.
MAKES: 2 DOZEN

INGREDIENTS

- 24 baby portobello mushrooms (about 1 pound), stems removed
- ½ cup reduced-fat mayonnaise
- ¾ cup shredded Asiago cheese
- ½ cup loosely packed basil leaves, stems removed
- ¼ teaspoon white pepper
- 12 cherry tomatoes, halved
-     Grated Parmesan cheese, optional

DIRECTIONS

1. Preheat oven to 375°. Place mushroom caps in a greased 15x10x1-in. baking pan. Bake 10 minutes. Meanwhile, place mayonnaise, Asiago cheese, basil and pepper in a food processor; process until mixture is blended.
2. Drain juices from mushrooms. Fill each cap with 1 rounded teaspoon mayonnaise mixture; top each with a tomato half.
3. Bake 8-10 minutes or until lightly browned. If desired, top with Parmesan cheese.

Mom's Garlic Pork Roast

PREP: 10 MIN.
BAKE: 1 HOUR 15 MIN. + STANDING
MAKES: 8 SERVINGS

INGREDIENTS

½ cup chopped celery
½ medium green pepper, finely chopped
½ cup thinly sliced green onions
8 garlic cloves, minced
1 bone-in pork loin roast (5 pounds)
1 teaspoon salt
¼ teaspoon cayenne pepper

DIRECTIONS

1. Preheat oven to 350°. In a small bowl, mix celery, green pepper, green onions and garlic.
2. Place roast in a roasting pan, fat side up. With a sharp knife, make deep slits into top of roast, cutting between ribs. Fill slits with the vegetable mixture. Sprinkle roast with salt and cayenne.
3. Roast until meat reaches desired doneness (for medium-rare, a thermometer should read 145°; medium, 160°), 1¼ to 1½ hours. Remove roast from oven; tent with foil. Let stand 15 minutes before carving roast.

Turkey Wild Rice Soup

PREP: 10 MIN. • **COOK:** 35 MIN.
MAKES: 12 SERVINGS (ABOUT 3 QUARTS)

INGREDIENTS

½ cup butter, cubed
2 carrots, finely chopped
2 celery ribs, finely chopped
1 medium onion, chopped
½ cup all-purpose flour
4 cups chicken or turkey broth
2 cups cooked wild rice
2 cups cubed cooked turkey
2 cups half-and-half cream
1 teaspoon dried parsley flakes
½ teaspoon salt
¼ teaspoon pepper

DIRECTIONS

1. In a Dutch oven, heat butter over medium-high heat. Add carrots, celery and onion; cook and stir until tender.
2. Stir in flour until blended; cook until bubbly. Gradually stir in broth. Bring to a boil, stirring constantly; cook and stir 1-2 minutes or until the mixture is thickened.
3. Stir in remaining ingredients; return to a boil. Reduce heat; simmer, uncovered, for 20 minutes, stirring occasionally.

Hot Cider Punch

PREP: 5 MIN. • **COOK:** 30 MIN.
MAKES: 12 SERVINGS

INGREDIENTS

- 3½ cups apple cider or juice
- 2 tablespoons sugar
- 1 cinnamon stick (3 inches)
- ½ teaspoon ground nutmeg
- 3 cups orange juice
- 3 cups unsweetened pineapple juice
- 1 teaspoon whole cloves
- 1 medium orange, cut into wedges

DIRECTIONS

1. Place cider, sugar, cinnamon stick and nutmeg in a large saucepan; bring to a boil. Reduce heat; simmer, covered, 20 minutes.
2. Stir in orange and pineapple juices. Insert cloves into orange wedges; add to cider mixture and heat through. Discard cinnamon stick. Serve warm.

Standing Rib Roast

PREP: 5 MIN. • **BAKE:** 2¼ HOURS + STANDING
MAKES: 10 SERVINGS

INGREDIENTS

- 3 teaspoons lemon-pepper seasoning
- 3 teaspoons paprika
- 1½ teaspoons garlic salt
- 1 teaspoon dried rosemary, crushed
- ½ teaspoon cayenne pepper
- 1 bone-in beef rib roast (6 to 7 pounds)
- 2 cups beef stock

DIRECTIONS

1. Preheat oven to 325°. In a small bowl, mix the first five ingredients. Place roast in a roasting pan, fat side up; rub with seasoning mixture.
2. Roast 2¼ to 2¾ hours or until meat reaches desired doneness (for medium-rare, a thermometer should read 145°; medium, 160°; well-done, 170°). Remove roast from oven; tent with foil. Let stand 15 minutes before carving.
3. Meanwhile, pour drippings and loosened browned bits from roasting pan into a small saucepan. Skim fat. Add beef stock to drippings; bring to a boil. Serve with roast.

Citrus Cranberry Pie

PREP: 30 MIN. • **BAKE:** 50 MIN. • **MAKES:** 8 SERVINGS

INGREDIENTS

- 3½ cups fresh or frozen cranberries
- 1 cup sugar
- 2 teaspoons grated lemon peel
- 1 teaspoon grated orange peel
- 1 small navel orange, peeled, sectioned and chopped
- 2 tablespoons butter, melted
- 4 teaspoons all-purpose flour
- ¼ teaspoon salt
  Pastry for double-crust pie (9 inches)
- 1 large egg, lightly beaten
  Additional sugar

ORANGE CREAM

- 1 cup heavy whipping cream
- 1 tablespoon sugar
- 2 teaspoons grated orange peel
- ½ teaspoon orange extract, optional

DIRECTIONS

1. Preheat oven to 450°. Toss together first eight ingredients.

2. On a lightly floured surface, roll one half of pastry dough to a ⅛-in.-thick circle; transfer to a 9-in. pie plate. Trim pastry even with rim. Add filling.

3. Roll remaining dough to a ⅛-in.-thick circle; cut into strips. Arrange over filling in a lattice pattern. Trim and seal strips to edge of bottom pastry; flute edge. Brush lattice with egg; sprinkle with additional sugar. Cover edges loosely with foil.

4. Bake 10 minutes. Reduce oven setting to 350°. Remove foil; bake until golden brown, for 40-45 minutes. Cool on a wire rack.

5. Meanwhile, beat whipping cream until it begins to thicken. Add remaining ingredients; beat until soft peaks form. Refrigerate until serving. Serve with pie.

PASTRY FOR DOUBLE-CRUST PIE (9 INCHES): Mix 2½ cups all-purpose flour and ½ tsp. salt; cut in 1 cup cold butter until crumbly. Gradually add ⅓ to ⅔ cup ice water, tossing with a fork until dough holds together when pressed. Divide dough in half. Shape each into a disk; wrap in plastic. Refrigerate 1 hour or overnight.

Peppermint Brownie Cups

PREP: 40 MIN. • **BAKE:** 15 MIN./BATCH + COOLING • **MAKES:** 4 DOZEN

INGREDIENTS

- 1 cup butter, cubed
- 1 cup plus 3 tablespoons milk chocolate chips
- 3 ounces unsweetened chocolate, chopped
- 3 large eggs
- 1¼ cups sugar
- 1 tablespoon instant coffee granules
- 2 teaspoons vanilla extract
- ½ teaspoon peppermint extract
- ⅔ cup all-purpose flour
- 1½ teaspoons baking powder
- ½ teaspoon salt

FROSTING

- 1½ cups confectioners' sugar
- 1 cup butter, softened
- 1 teaspoon peppermint extract
- 1 jar (7 ounces) marshmallow creme
  Peppermint crunch baking chips

DIRECTIONS

1. Preheat oven to 350°. Line 48 mini-muffin cups with paper liners or foil liners.
2. In a metal bowl over simmering water, melt butter, chocolate chips and unsweetened chocolate; stir until smooth. Cool slightly.
3. In a large bowl, beat eggs, sugar and coffee granules until blended. Stir in the extracts and chocolate mixture. In another bowl, whisk the flour, baking powder and salt; gradually add to chocolate mixture, mixing well.
4. Fill prepared cups three-fourths full. Bake 12-14 minutes or until a toothpick inserted in center comes out clean (do not overbake). Cool in pans 5 minutes before removing to wire racks to cool completely.
5. For frosting, in a small bowl, beat confectioners' sugar, butter and extract until smooth. Fold in the marshmallow creme. Pipe or spread frosting over brownie cups; sprinkle with peppermint baking chips.

Coconut Slice & Bake Cookies

PREP: 25 MIN. + CHILLING
BAKE: 15 MIN./BATCH
MAKES: ABOUT 4½ DOZEN

INGREDIENTS

- 3 cups flaked coconut, divided
- 15 drops red food coloring
- 10 drops green food coloring
- 1 cup butter, softened
- ¾ cup sugar
- 2 cups all-purpose flour

DIRECTIONS

1. Place 1 cup coconut in each of two large resealable plastic bags. Add the red food coloring to one bag; seal bag and shake to tint coconut. Repeat with the remaining coconut and green food coloring.
2. In a large bowl, cream butter and sugar until light and fluffy; gradually beat in flour. Stir in remaining coconut. Divide the dough in half.
3. Shape one portion of dough into a 7-in.-long log; roll in red coconut, pressing firmly to help adhere. Wrap in plastic wrap. Repeat with remaining dough and green coconut. Refrigerate 1-2 hours or until firm.
4. Preheat oven to 325°. Unwrap and cut dough crosswise into ¼-in. slices. Place 1 in. apart on ungreased baking sheets. Bake 12-14 minutes or until the bottoms are light brown. Remove from pans to wire racks to cool.

Handcrafted with Love

Bales of Holiday Cheer

These straw gifts say someone's on the Nice List this year.

WHAT YOU'LL NEED

- Choice of straw bales
- Choice of fabric
- 3-in.-wide wire ribbon
- Safety pins
- Pinking shears (optional)

DIRECTIONS

1. Cut fabric pieces to desired width according to size of straw bales. Wrap a fabric piece centered around each hay bale. Overlap fabric slightly on bottom of bale and secure in place with safety pins.

2. Wrap each straw bale with wire ribbon, cutting ends with pinking shears if desired to prevent fraying. Tie ribbon on top and finish with a bow. Stack bales on a porch or in the yard.

Rope Them In

Twist it, tie it and welcome guests home for the holidays.

WHAT YOU'LL NEED

- 62 ft. of ½-in.-wide sisal twisted rope
- 14-in.-wide wire wreath frame
- 22-gauge floral wire
- Choice of decorations such as florals and greenery
- Utility knife
- Wire cutters
- Hot glue gun

DIRECTIONS

1. Use utility knife to cut four 1-yd. lengths of rope; set rope aside for Step 4.

2. Place wire wreath frame flat to work. Layer most of the remaining 50 ft. of rope in circular loops on top of frame.

3. With about 6 ft. of rope remaining, create a double hanging loop at top of wreath. Wrap remainder of rope tightly around itself and the wire frame backing. Secure hanging loop to back side with a clove hitch or simple knot. Apply hot glue to end of the rope; knot to secure in place and prevent fraying.

4. In 4 symmetrically placed points on the wreath, wrap 1 of the remaining 1-yd. pieces tightly around the ropes and wire frame. (See photo at left as a guide.) Secure each wrapped piece in place with a knot on the back side of the wreath. Use hot glue to prevent fraying.

5. Use wire cutters to cut several segments of floral wire. Attach layered strands of rope to wire frame using floral wire segments. Secure in at least 6 places around the back side of the frame, making sure the rope does not sag.

6. Use hot glue to attach decorations such as silk flowers, mistletoe, freshly cut evergreen or holly branches.

NOTE This weight of rope is easy to work with, but may sag if not fastened well to a strong wire wreath frame.

Lucky Season

Bright-colored berries deck out a horseshoe with a little yuletide magic.

WHAT YOU'LL NEED

- Horseshoe
- 6 yds. or more of heavy twine
- Choice of greenery for decoration
- Large jingle bell
- Hot glue gun
- Floral wire (optional)

DIRECTIONS

1. Cut five 1-yd. strands of heavy twine.

2. Thread 2 strands of twine through one hole on the side of horseshoe. Line up strand ends. Tie gathered strands in a double knot flush against back side of the horseshoe. Using 1 strand on each outer side and 2 combined strands in the middle, braid the twine. Stop about halfway along the length, leaving strands loose at the end.

3. Repeat process above in a hole on other side of horseshoe to create 2 matching braided sections of twine.

4. Thread the last 1-yd. strand of twine through the jingle bell and line up ends.

5. Gather all strands together. At the end of the braided sections, tie a knot to secure all strands in place. (The jingle bell should now hang centered in the horseshoe.) Then divide the strands into 3 sections and braid together until about an 8-in. length remains loose.

6. To create the hanger, gather the remaining 8-in. length of strands together. Use a new length of twine and coil it tightly around all the gathered strands, covering completely. Form a loop from the 8-in. length of covered strands. Place end of the coiled loop overlapping top of braided section. Continue tightly coiling twine around loop end and top of braided section to secure the hanger in place. Trim ends and tie twine in a double knot on back side of hanger base. Use hot glue on the back side to further secure in place and prevent the twine from fraying.

7. Use hot glue or floral wire to attach choice of greenery or other decoration as desired. Hang on wall or door.

NOTE Horseshoes come in a variety of sizes and designs. Some have more than 1 hole on each side. If desired, thread and weave twine through all holes in the horseshoe design.

Indexes

FIND YOUR FAVORITE CRAFTS AND RECIPES EASILY.

"Of all the paths you take in life, make sure a few of them are dirt."
—John Muir